Amanda Riley made her first dress in 1976 on her grandmother's Singer sewing machine. She was 8 years old and she was hooked. By the age of 14 Amanda had her own small business making clothing for friends and family and at 16 she took part in her first fashion show in the local town hall. The collection sold out in minutes.

After completing her degree in fashion and textiles at Kingston University and following a career as a designer in Milan, Hong Kong and the US, Amanda stepped back from the main-stream fashion industry, due to her growing disaffection with its harmful effects on both the planet and society. As an antidote, Amanda started The Fashion Factory in 2009.

Amanda's sewing classes at The Fashion Factory are different, cool and fun – a far cry from the dreaded needlework classes of old. Amanda's approach is to encourage students to look at styles and trends, fashion and textiles, and pick something wearable and unique to make for themselves. She starts with the 'look' and makes the practical techniques simple and approachable. This easy and creative style means that demand for her courses is huge and waiting lists are full.

There is no other fashion school like The Fashion Factory and the last summer catwalk show was featured on Vogue.com.

the
FASHION FACTORY

the FASHION FACTORY

DESIGN, CREATE
AND SEW YOUR OWN
UNIQUE CLOTHES

AMANDA RILEY

QUADRILLE

CONTENTS

WELCOME TO THE FASHION FACTORY

The Fashion Factory is full of creative, fun and on-trend ideas for budding fashionistas who, no matter what their budget or where they live, can escape the uniformity of the high street to design and make their own unique clothes.

Aren't you bored of the high street? With every shop offering the same looks in cheap fabrics that fade or bobble after just a few washes, it's time to try something new. It's time to make yourself unique.

With practical projects and inspiring design ideas, this book is for anyone hankering to develop their own individual fashion style. The girls you see in the photographs throughout this book are all students at The Fashion Factory, past and present, who have made and modelled their own clothes to inspire you to become your own fashion designer.

You don't need to be an expert sewer to join The Fashion Factory. This book starts with the easiest projects and, as you work through the pages, progresses to a more advanced level. Every stage of the different projects is

broken down and clearly explained in both words and pictures. If you stay focused and are patient, you should be able to follow all the instructions very easily.

Don't worry if your first sewn garment is not perfect. The more you sew, the better results you will get. The methods I use are often not the 'professional' ways of making; rather they have been adapted and simplified so that beginners and young sewers can learn to make creatively without worrying too much about perfection. I believe learning should be a fun process, so sometimes I have ditched precision methods in favour of quick and easy sewing.

You can use recycled or second-hand materials for most of the projects in this book. This is a great way to keep your costs down while you are learning to sew. Often the finished garment is a whole lot more exciting when it's made from something old. Go to carboot sales and charity shops to buy up old T-shirts and denim jeans; they're cheap to buy and always look great once they are re-made into new designs. Plus we are all aware of the negative effect 'fast fashion' is having on the environment.

Once you've made something amazing, your friends will doubtless want you to make a version for them, too. Go for it. You'll find that the more you make, the faster you will get and the easier it will become and before you know it, everyone will be asking. If you are part of a group of friends who all want to learn to sew, then starting your own sewing group or 'sewing bee' is great fun.

Sharing your makes is one of the most satisfying parts of sewing. You will feel great when someone asks you where you got that fantastic dress or top you're wearing and you can say, 'I made it myself'.

Log onto Instagram and check out @TheFashionFactory.UK to see what we've been sewing recently. Share your sewing with the world by posting your completed designs onto The Fashion Factory Facebook page or sharing your makes on your own Instagram feed with the hashtag #thefashionfactory.

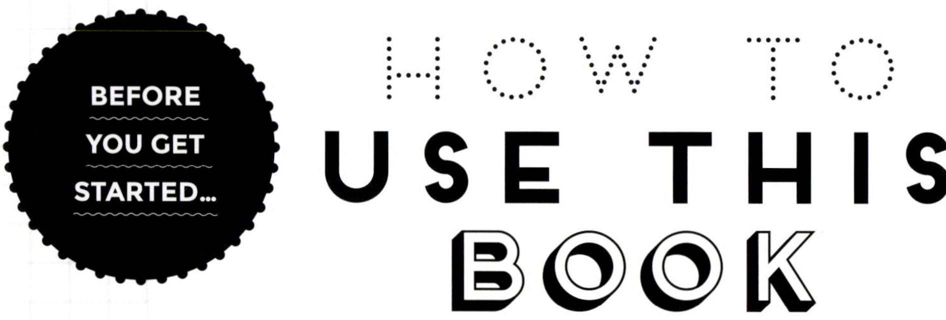

This book contains projects for various levels of sewing ability. You see that under the heading of each project there is a difficulty rating. Level 1 projects are the easiest. Level 2 projects are intermediate. Level 3 projects are more advanced. The best way for everyone to use this book is to start with the level 1 projects, before progressing to level 2 and level 3 projects.

If you're an advanced sewer, look out for the key words written in capitals throughout the instructions. These key words are highlighted in every project so that more advanced sewers or sewing teachers can quickly skim through each step.

Each step has been broken down very precisely so that anyone over 10 years old should be able to understand the instructions with ease. You'll find lots of reminders for all the key techniques and there are photographs to accompany the step-by-step instructions.

Fill in the chart on page 14 with your measurements so that you can refer to them each time you want to make yourself something new. There is also a section that will teach you how to make your own simple paper patterns. Once you've cut out your fabric pieces, you can refer to the design sections of the book and have some fun adding your own unique ideas. There you will find plenty of inspiration and ideas to achieve a whole wardrobe full of cool and stylish clothes. But most importantly, have some fun while you sew!

There is a FULL-SIZE PATTERN SHEET that accompanies this book. You'll need to know your measurements before you can use it. I recommend that you take your key measurements (see page 14) first and then TRACE OFF the correct size pattern for you onto DRESSMAKER'S PATTERN PAPER. Keep the original pattern sheet intact for future use. (You may well grow or you may want to make something in another size for a friend.)

BUYING A SEWING MACHINE

All sewing machines are different. I strongly advise that you do NOT go overboard on gadgets and gimmicks. The more a machine can do, the more there is to go wrong. Go for a respected brand that can sew STRETCH fabrics as well as WOVEN fabrics (see pages 24–5).

Sewing stretch fabrics is really easy and is great for beginners. Stretch fabrics do not FRAY (come unravelled at the edges), so that means you don't need to finish off or strengthen the fabric edges with stitching and your projects can be made more quickly. They are also easy to wear and if you grow they stretch to fit, so the garment may last longer.

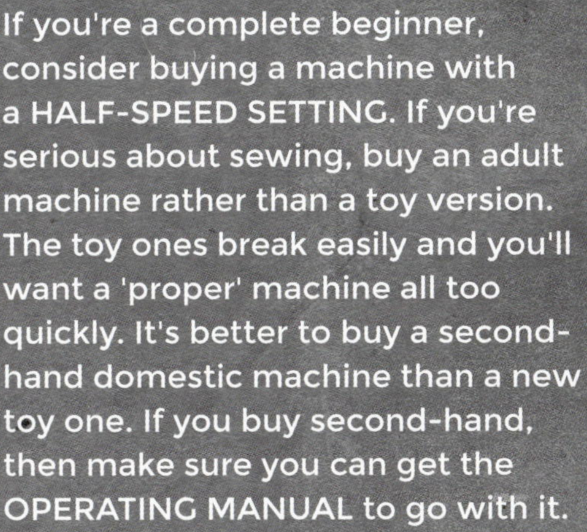

If you're a complete beginner, consider buying a machine with a HALF-SPEED SETTING. If you're serious about sewing, buy an adult machine rather than a toy version. The toy ones break easily and you'll want a 'proper' machine all too quickly. It's better to buy a second-hand domestic machine than a new toy one. If you buy second-hand, then make sure you can get the OPERATING MANUAL to go with it.

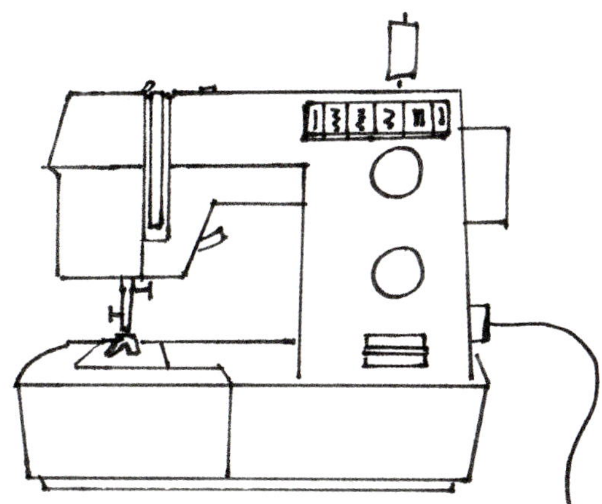

GETTING TO KNOW YOUR SEWING MACHINE

If you already have a sewing machine, make sure you also have the OPERATING MANUAL to go with it. If you don't, buy a copy online (eBay is a good source). Studying your manual is invaluable because it shows you clearly how to THREAD UP your machine and WIND A BOBBIN. It's essential that you know how to do both these things properly before you start sewing (see pages 26–9).

Remember to CLEAN your sewing machine every few months: you'll be amazed at how many problems are caused by bits of fluff stuck inside. Go through the manual and follow the steps on how to clean your machine before sewing. If it's playing up, treat your machine to a FULL SERVICE at your local sewing-machine centre.

A HAPPY MACHINE makes for a HAPPY SEWING experience. If your sewing machine is missing stitches or not sewing correctly, go to the TROUBLESHOOTING tips on page 36.

Always use the correct size and type of needle in your sewing machine for the fabric you are using (see page 17). Also replace your sewing needle for every new project as blunt needles can cause your sewing machine to skip stitches.

ESSENTIAL SEWING EQUIPMENT

MEASURING TAPE

DRESSMAKING PINS

TAILOR'S CHALK

PENCIL

STITCH RIPPER

FIBRE-TIP PEN

★ Sewing machine
★ Assorted sewing machine needles
★ Hand sewing needles
★ Dressmaker's pattern paper or large sheets of thin paper
★ Set square
★ Steam iron
★ Ironing board

TAKING YOUR KEY MEASUREMENTS

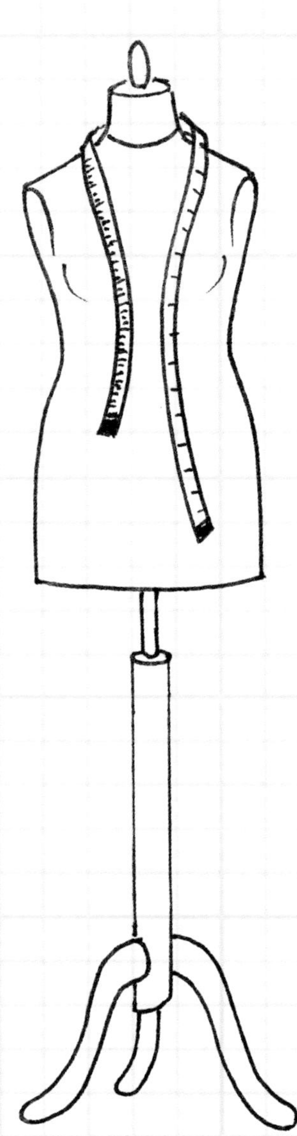

It's important to take some body measurements in order to make properly fitting clothes. Measure yourself at the following points in centimetres:

A Chest – measure around your chest and across your bust at the WIDEST point

B Waist – measure around your waist at the NARROWEST point

C Hip – measure around your hips and across your bottom at the WIDEST point

○ Measure yourself over your underwear, not over thick clothing.

○ Check that you are starting from the correct end of your measuring tape.

○ Stand in front of a full-length mirror so that you get the measuring tape in the right place.

○ When you take the measurements, keep the measuring tape horizontal.

○ Don't pull your measuring tape too tight and don't breathe in – just relax.

○ Ask someone else to help if you're having trouble.

Before you start sewing, fill your measurements into the boxes opposite. Keep these measurements on hand for reference every time you want to make a new garment – that way, you won't have to keep measuring yourself as you go along.

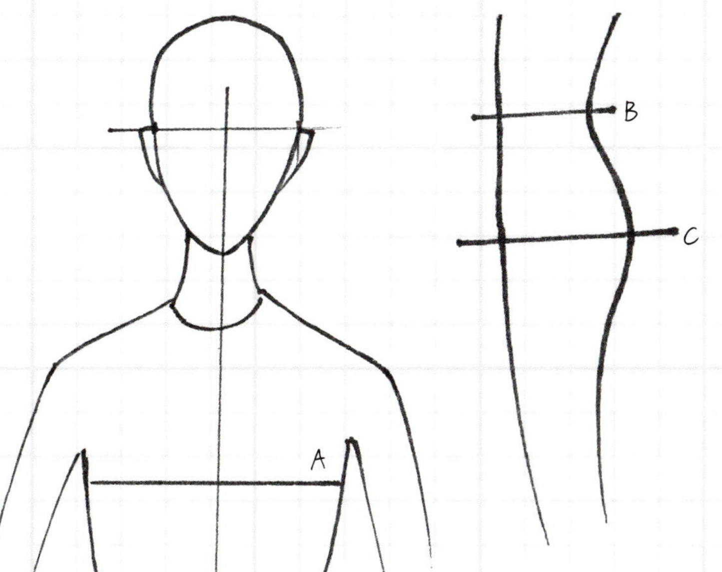

Fill in your measurements in the first box below, then go to the second box to work out which size to use from the pattern sheet that accompanies this book.

	your measurement in cm
CHEST	
WAIST	
HIP	

your chest size (cm)	use pattern size
71–75cm	1
77–81cm	2
82–86cm	3
87–91cm	4
92–96cm	5

YOU WILL NEED

- ○ Dressmaker's pattern paper (available from haberdashers or online) or large sheets of thin plain paper like craft paper or newsprint (without ink)
- ○ Measuring tape
- ○ Sticky tape (masking tape or electrical tape is best as it's easy to peel off)
- ○ Paper scissors
- ○ Long ruler
- ○ Fibre-tip pen
- ○ Pencil
- ○ Pins
- ○ Set square or something with a 90 degree corner to draw round
- ○ Large work table

✶✶✶✶✶✶✶✶✶✶✶✶✶✶✶✶✶✶✶✶✶✶

If you don't want to buy pattern paper, then you could use large sheets of any kind of thin paper, newsprint (not newspaper as the ink can transfer onto your fabric), craft paper or even wrapping paper.

MAKING YOUR OWN BASIC SKIRT PATTERN

This is the method that you need to use for ALL the skirt shapes in this book. It's a very easy and useful method of pattern cutting called the SPLIT AND SPREAD METHOD. This method is used anywhere where FLARE and FULLNESS is required in a garment, such as SKIRTS and DRESSES, PEPLUM TOPS and SKIRTS, SLEEVES, and FRILLS and RUFFLES

It only involves calculating a couple of measurements – don't worry if you hate maths, this is very simple.

MEASURE your WAIST in centimetres (see page 14). Do not breathe in and do not pull the measuring tape too tight. DIVIDE this measurement by 2. Call this Measurement A.

If you're making the Flared Skater Dress, GO TO the Flared Skater Dress section on page 21 for Measurement A.

Now DECIDE on the LENGTH that you would like the skirt to be. MEASURE from your waist down. Do not make the skirt length too short. You will shorten the skirt once it's finished. Call this Measurement B.

That's all the measuring done.

MEASUREMENT A = circumference of waist in cm ÷ 2

MEASUREMENT B = length of skirt from waist in cm

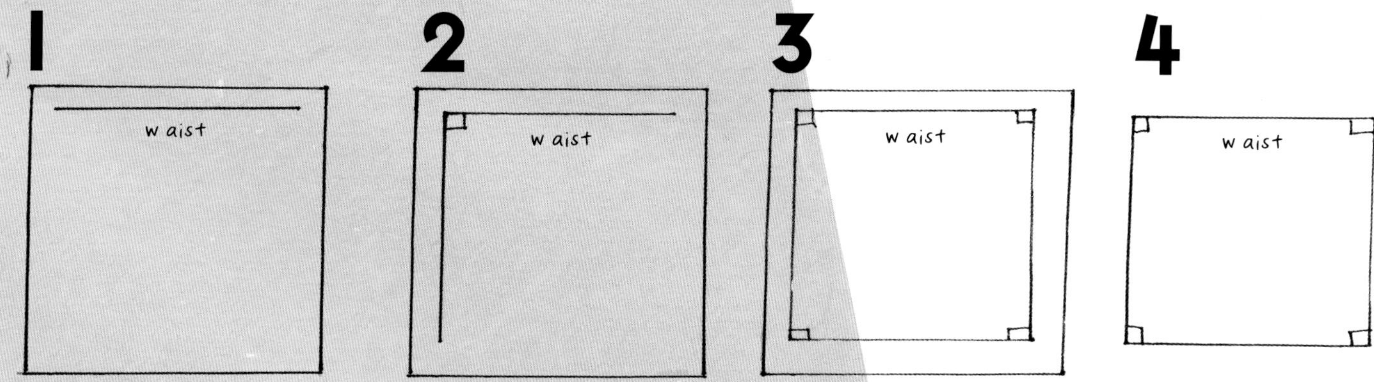

MAKING THE BASIC SKIRT BLOCK

1. Take a large sheet of paper. Along the top edge and using a ruler, DRAW a STRAIGHT LINE the length of Measurement A. Write the word 'WAIST' just below this line.

2. DRAW a STRAIGHT LINE the length of Measurement B at a right angle (90 degrees) to the waist line. If you have one, use a set square for a perfect right angle.

3. CREATE a BOX by drawing two more lines. Make sure all the corners are at right angles.

4. Carefully CUT OUT your shape.

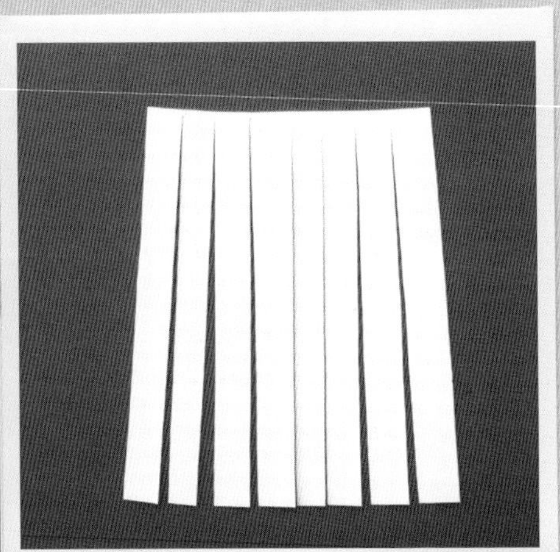

Make vertical cuts in pattern piece at regular intervals.

5

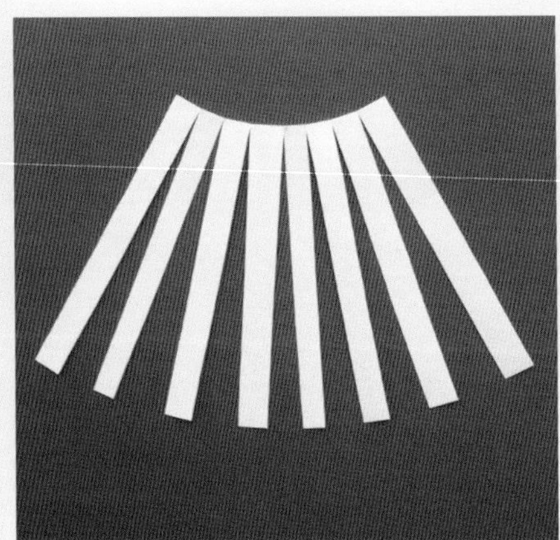

Place 'split' pattern piece on second sheet of paper.

5 Now it's time for the 'split' part. Using paper scissors, make VERTICAL CUTS in your pattern piece at REGULAR INTERVALS, seven or eight times. Cut from the bottom almost to the top. LEAVE a THREAD-LIKE amount at the top (literally 2–3mm) to act as a HINGE. Try not to rip the paper at the hinges. If you do, use a little sticky tape to rejoin.

6 Take a second large sheet of paper. PLACE the SPLIT PATTERN piece ON TOP.

7 Now evenly SPREAD OUT the cut sections into a FAN SHAPE. The further you spread these sections out, the more 'flared' or 'full' your skirt will be (and the more fabric you will need as the shape gets bigger). Make sure you KEEP a nice EVEN CURVE at the waist.

8 When you're happy with the skirt shape, gently PRESS DOWN the little PAPER HINGES at the top, keeping them flat. Use tiny bits of sticky tape to fix your shape down in several places.

Look after your paper patterns so that you can use them again and again. Fold the pattern pieces neatly and store them in large envelopes. Draw a sketch of the garment on the envelope so that you know at a glance which pattern is inside.

7

Fan out sections, keeping smooth curve at waist.

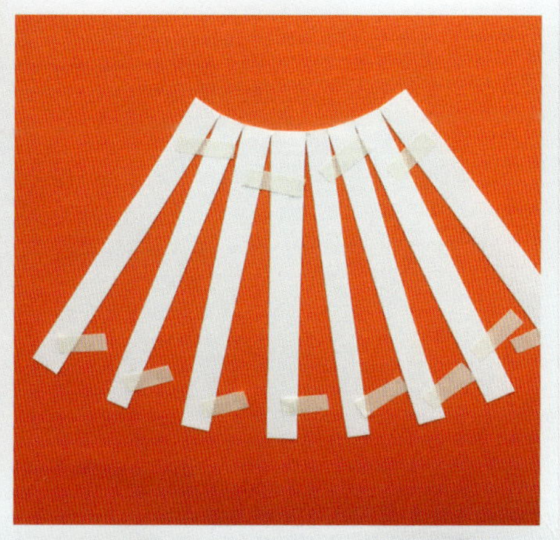

Press down paper hinges and fix shape with sticky tape.

Draw around outline of split sections, creating smooth curves.

(9) Using a fibre-tip pen, DRAW a HEAVY LINE round your skirt shape. DRAW along the edges of your curves, both top and bottom. The line should be a nice SMOOTH CURVE that just touches the CENTRE of each panel.

Carefully PEEL OFF the top 'split and spread' piece. This is your BASIC SKIRT BLOCK for the design you're about to create.

The further you 'spread' the sections apart, the more 'flared' or 'full' your skirt will be (and the more fabric you'll need as the shape gets bigger).

MAKING THE BASIC WAISTBAND BLOCK

If you're making the Colour Block Skater Skirt, Twirly 'Art' Skirt or Denim Dungaree Dress, you need to make the waistband pattern.

Using a ruler, draw a straight line the length of Measurement A.

Draw another line at each end. Both must be 10cm long and at a right angle to the first line.

Join the lines to make a rectangle.

Carefully cut around the outer lines.

Now go to your chosen skirt or dress project instructions to add any necessary seam allowances or adjustments.

10cm

waistband

A

I

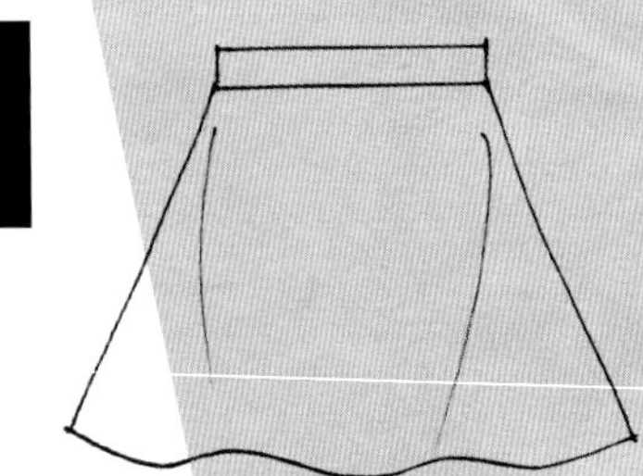

PATTERN 1: COLOUR BLOCK SKATER SKIRT

Take your BASIC SKIRT BLOCK and, using a ruler, add a 1cm SEAM ALLOWANCE all the way round.

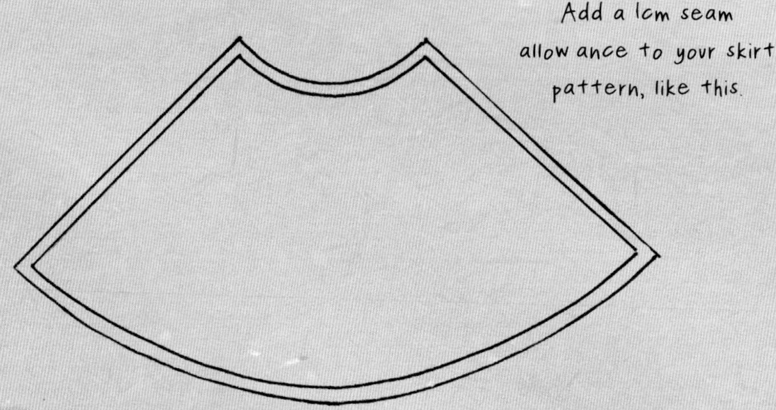

Be very precise when adding seam allowances to your pattern pieces. Always use a ruler.

CUT OUT your pattern along the outer line.

For an extra simple skirt style, CUT TWO SKIRT PANELS in stretch fabric only.

For a four-panel skirt, FOLD the pattern piece IN HALF so that the top corners meet. MAKE a sharp CREASE down the CENTRE.

CUT the pattern into TWO HALVES along the crease line.

Take ONE of these halves. Write CENTRE along the cut edge. You will need to cut out four of these panels in stretch fabric.

You don't need to make any changes to the waistband pattern block you made earlier, so cut it out and use it as it is. Now GO TO PAGE 50 to learn how to cut out and make your Colour Block Skater Skirt.

2

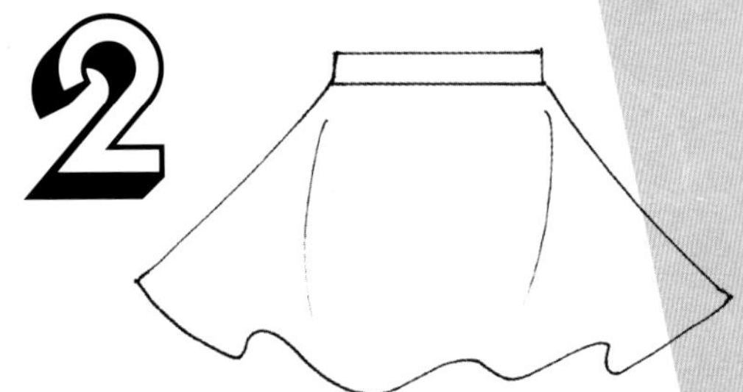

PATTERN 2: TWIRLY ART SKIRT

Take your BASIC SKIRT BLOCK and WAISTBAND BLOCK. Using a ruler, add a 1.5cm SEAM ALLOWANCE all the way round both pattern pieces.

Carefully CUT OUT the pattern pieces.

Now GO TO PAGE 86 to learn how to make your Twirly 'Art' Skirt.

PATTERN 3: FLARED SKATER DRESS

If you're making the Flared Skater Dress, your skirt panels must fit the width of your bodice. You'll USE PATTERN A on the sheet that comes with this book for the bodice, so find your size (see pages 14–15). On the two bodice pattern pieces, you'll see a FOLD LINE near the bottom of the bodices. MEASURE the total length of the FOLD LINE on the FRONT and BACK BODICE pieces. That is Measurement A.

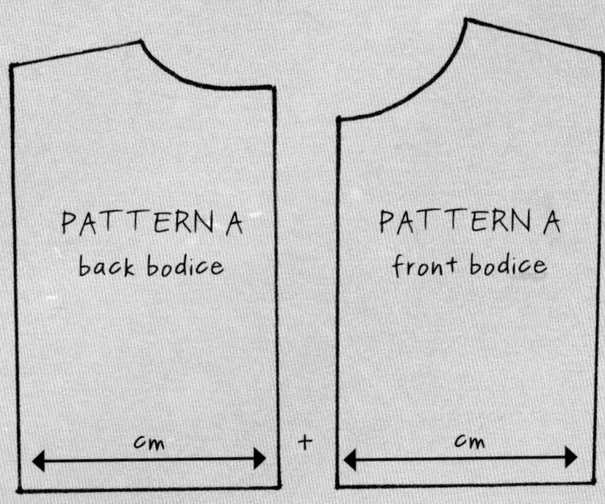

MEASUREMENT A = width of front bodice + width of back bodice

Now GO BACK TO MAKING A BASIC SKIRT BLOCK at step 2 on page 17 and continue making your skirt pattern.

When you've made your pattern, GO TO PAGE 106 to learn how to cut out and make your Flared Skater Dress.

If you want to re-use any paper patterns that you make, I recommend buying proper dressmaker's pattern paper. You can buy this by the metre at your local haberdashers or online. Pattern paper has a grid drawn on it – made up of dots or letters or numbers – and is very thin so it is great for tracing. This grid helps to keep everything symmetrical and lined up. It also helps you to place your pattern correctly on your fabric.

PATTERN 4: DENIM DUNGAREE DRESS

Take your BASIC SKIRT BLOCK and WAISTBAND BLOCK. Using a ruler, add a 1.5cm SEAM ALLOWANCE all the way round both pieces.

Carefully CUT OUT the pattern pieces.

GO TO PAGE 134 to learn how to cut out and make your Denim Dungaree Dress.

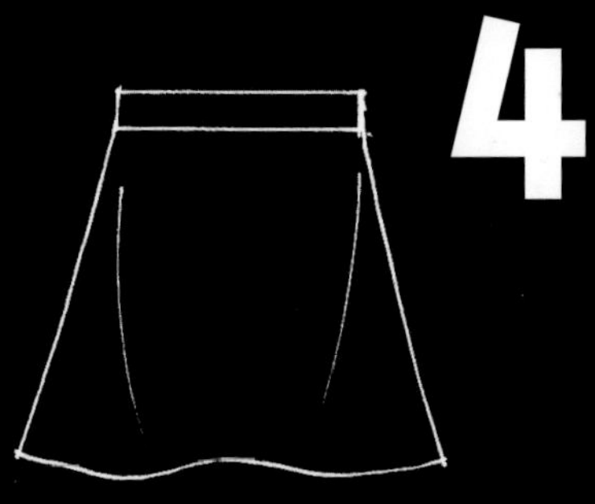

4

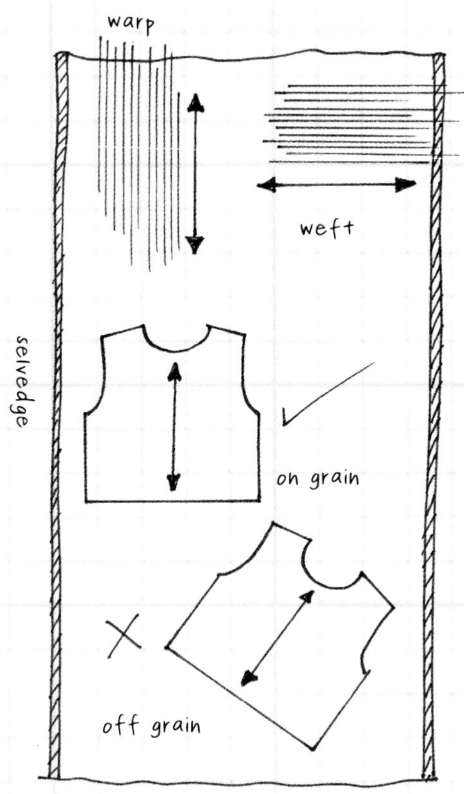

PREPARING TO SEW

PLACING YOUR PAPER PATTERN ON THE FABRIC (ON GRAIN)

If you've bought new fabric, you'll see that it has two cut ends but that the sides look different. The FINISHED EDGES that run up and down the length of the fabric are called SELVEDGES. This is where the fabric was fixed onto the machine that made it. It's important to identify and know where your selvedges are before you start cutting out a garment.

The threads or fibres that run from selvedge to selvedge (or right to left across the fabric) are called the WEFT threads. The threads or fibres that run up and down are called the WARP threads. The CENTRE LINE of your pattern piece must be placed EXACTLY on either the WARP or WEFT of your fabric so that your garment will hang correctly. This is called placing the pattern piece ON GRAIN. It is on the grain of your fabric when it is lined up with the warp or weft threads.

If you're recycling and can't see a selvedge, then place your CENTRE LINE exactly in line with your warp or weft threads so that it is ON THE GRAIN of the fabric. If you look very closely at your fabric, you should be able to see the warp and weft threads.

PINNING YOUR GARMENT FOR STITCHING

Try to copy the direction of the pins in the step-by-step photographs. You'll either sew towards the point of the pins (so that you can slide them out from in front of the presser foot as you go along) or you'll sew over the top of the pin shaft sideways. So look carefully at the photographs and note the pin direction.

NEVER LEAVE YOUR HOT IRON UNATTENDED OR THE HOTPLATE ON THE SURFACE OF YOUR FABRIC FOR TOO LONG.

USING YOUR IRON

It's essential to press your seams as you make your garment. A steam iron is best. If you don't know how to use your iron then ASK AN ADULT TO HELP.

Fill the reservoir with water (but don't overfill it) and set it to the correct temperature for your fabric. Always TEST THE TEMPERATURE on a scrap of fabric before you begin to press. If the temperature is set too high, then you could melt or burn your fabric.

When sewing STRETCH FABRICS a steam iron is particularly useful. Stretch fabrics can become distorted and stretched when sewn, especially on hemlines. If this happens you can set your iron to FULL STEAM and hold it JUST ABOVE the SURFACE of your fabric. Lower the iron and press full steam as it gets closer to the cloth (keep your hands out of the way when you do this). The hot steam will SHRINK the fabric back to its original position.

CUTTING OUT

There's a skill to achieving accurate and smooth edges when cutting fabric. You must use very SHARP SCISSORS. Buy proper fabric shears, in the correct size for your hand, from a haberdashery or online. Holding the scissors the right way up, always cut fabric on a hard, flat surface. SLIDE the bottom blade along the table as you cut (it should never leave the table surface). Cut SLOWLY using the TIPS of the blades. As you become more practised, speed up and take bigger snips. Stay as close to your pattern as possible without cutting the paper. If you're right-handed cut in an anti-clockwise direction, the reverse if you're left-handed.

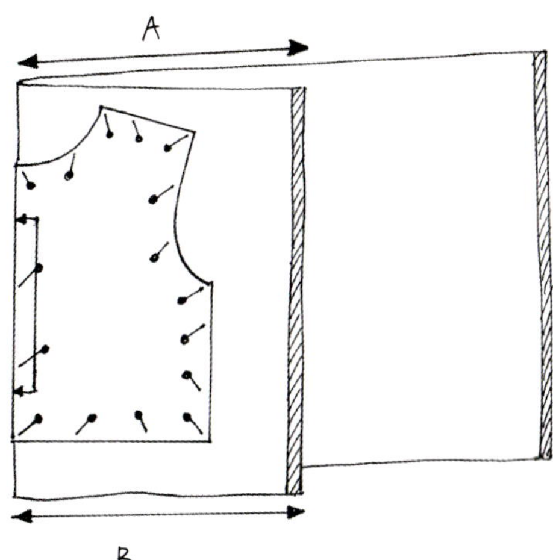

A and B should be equal lengths

PINNING YOUR PAPER PATTERN TO THE FABRIC

When pinning your paper pattern to the fabric, try to remember these few things:

- FOLD the FABRIC so that the SELVEDGE is PARALLEL to your FOLD. Use a measuring tape to check it's the same distance all the way down.
- Place the CENTRE LINE of your pattern piece EXACTLY on the FOLD LINE of the fabric.
- PIN the CENTRE LINE of your pattern piece FIRST, then the CORNERS.
- PIN DIAGONALLY into all the CORNERS, so that the fabric stays flat. Then pin into any curves.
- Always pin CURVES well.
- Always use sharp dressmaking pins. Don't use BLUNT pins as they could ruin your fabric.

BUYING FABRIC

For some of the projects in this book you might choose to buy new fabric rather than recycle something old, especially if it's a project that uses a stretch fabric. Most dress fabrics come in two different widths 115cm and 150cm. Some stretch fabrics are 200cm. Prepare your paper pattern before you shop for fabric so that you can work out how much you will need.

SEWING STRETCH FABRICS

You'll need the correct needle in your sewing machine (either a ballpoint needle or a stretch needle), so take a look at the chart on page 29 and insert the right type and size. Ensure that the flat part of the shaft is at the back and push in the needle as far as it will go.

If you have a machine that can handle stretch fabrics, then select a stretch stitch. Refer to your manual and find the STRAIGHT STRETCH STITCH or TRIPLE STRAIGHT STITCH. Once you've made the selection, try sewing a scrap of stretch fabric. You will see that the machine sews two stitches forwards and then one stitch backwards and repeats. This is so that the stitching can stretch along with the fabric when the garment is worn.

If your machine doesn't have a stretch stitch option, then select a small ZIGZAG STITCH. This will do the same job as a stretch stitch.

SEWING WOVEN FABRICS

You'll need a universal needle in your sewing machine, so again check the chart on page 29 to choose the correct size. Insert the needle with the flat part of the shaft at the back and push it in as far as it will go.

Select a regular STRAIGHT STITCH. Refer to your manual for how to do this. Test your straight stitch on a piece of scrap fabric before you start sewing your garment. Take a moment to check that the stitch tension and stitch length are both correct (see page 28).

NEW FABRICS

Once you've bought your fabric, wash and dry it before you cut out your garment pieces. Fabrics can shrink by up to 10% during washing.

As a beginner, avoid fabrics that are very fine like chiffons, silks or satins, as these are difficult to work with. Stick to cottons, denims and polyester/cotton or polyester/viscose blends.

WINDING YOUR BOBBIN

It's very important that your bobbin is properly filled. If it is not, then your stitching will be either too tight or too loose, or it will get caught up inside the sewing machine. NEVER USE A BAGGY BOBBIN! If you do, you will be heading for disaster. Follow the manual for your sewing machine very carefully. Your bobbin should be hard and solid when it's full of thread. Don't wind your bobbin at full speed until you have mastered the technique.

This is how I wind a bobbin on my machine. Yours may differ, so refer to your manual as well as reading my tips.

1. Place the sewing thread on the thread holder on your sewing machine. Put the thread cap on the end to stop the reel of thread from coming off.
2. The sewing thread should now pass around the thread guide from the back towards the front. (On my machine, this looks like a miniature cappuccino cup and saucer. I place the thread between the cup and the saucer.)
3. There is a tiny hole in the side of your empty bobbin. Pass the end of the sewing thread through this hole from the inside to the outside.
4. Place the bobbin on the bobbin pin, holding the end of the thread in place.
5. Pull out the handwheel (or unscrew it on older machines) to disengage the needle. This stops the needle from sewing madly when you're filling the bobbin.
6. Push the bobbin on the pin to the right or click in place.
7. Switch on the sewing machine. Hold the end of the thread tightly and gently press the foot peddle.
8. After the bobbin has turned just a few times, stop. Cut off the loose end.
9. Continue filling the bobbin until it automatically stops.
10. When it's full, push the bobbin on the pin to the left. Cut the thread, remove the bobbin from the winder and push in (or tighten) the handwheel.

TIP

Gently hold the thread to stop it from jumping out of the thread guide. If it does jump out, you'll have a baggy bobbin. NEVER USE A BAGGY BOBBIN! If you do, your machine won't sew correctly. When winding, watch the thread guide and not the bobbin to make sure that the thread doesn't jump out of the guide.

INSERTING A BOBBIN INTO A TOP-LOADING SEWING MACHINE

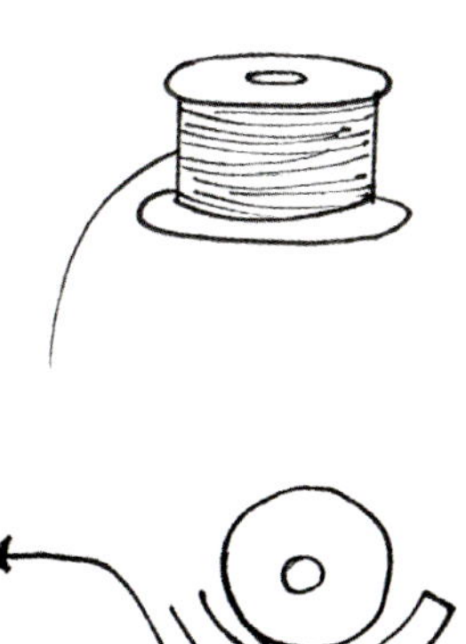

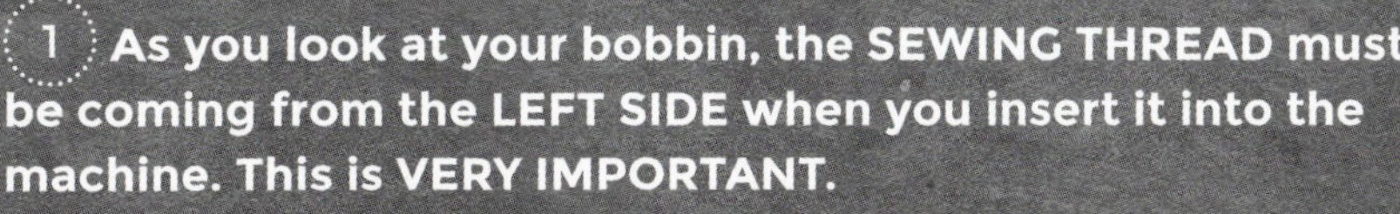

1 As you look at your bobbin, the SEWING THREAD must be coming from the LEFT SIDE when you insert it into the machine. This is VERY IMPORTANT.

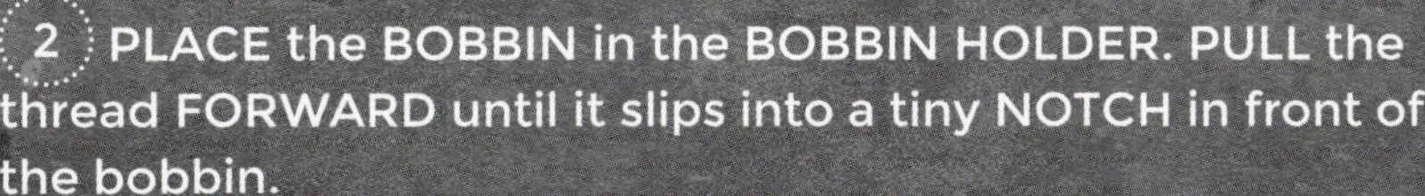

2 PLACE the BOBBIN in the BOBBIN HOLDER. PULL the thread FORWARD until it slips into a tiny NOTCH in front of the bobbin.

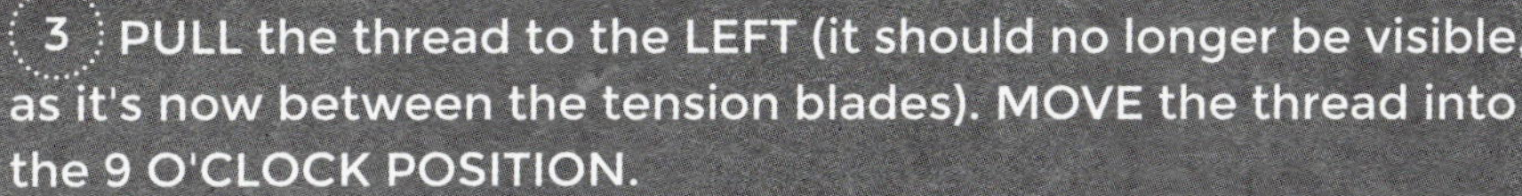

3 PULL the thread to the LEFT (it should no longer be visible, as it's now between the tension blades). MOVE the thread into the 9 O'CLOCK POSITION.

THREAD UP your sewing machine and then go to 'Bringing up the Bottom Thread' (see page 28).

NEVER USE A BAGGY BOBBIN!

INSERTING A BOBBIN INTO A FRONT-LOADING SEWING MACHINE WITH A BOBBIN CASE

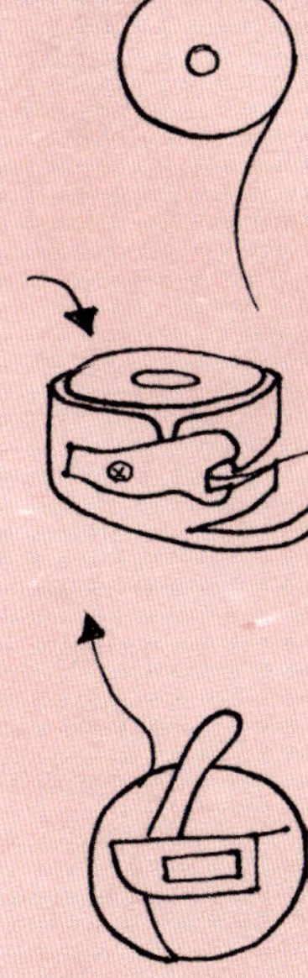

1 As you look at your bobbin, the SEWING THREAD must be coming from the RIGHT SIDE.

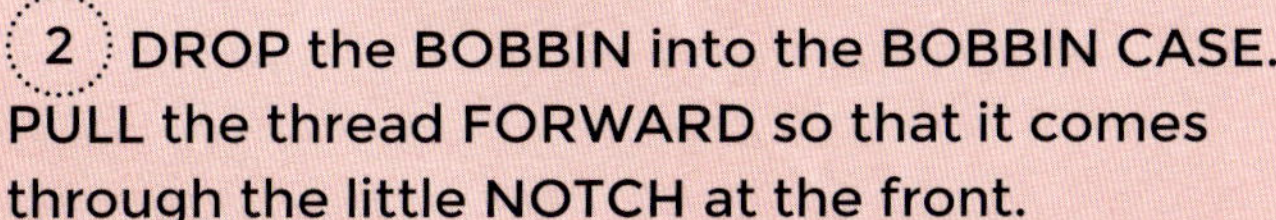

2 DROP the BOBBIN into the BOBBIN CASE. PULL the thread FORWARD so that it comes through the little NOTCH at the front.

3 PULL the thread to the RIGHT and DOWN until it clicks into place.

4 PULL the handle out, from underneath the BOBBIN CASE. Note the position of the thread. Keep HOLD of this HANDLE and, with the HOOK at the TOP, INSERT the BOBBIN CASE into place in the SEWING MACHINE.

THREAD UP your sewing machine and then go to 'Bringing up the Bottom Thread' (see page 28).

HELP WITH THREADING UP

The correct threading up of your sewing machine is essential. Carefully STUDY THE MANUAL or go online for a tutorial specifically for your machine type. If your sewing machine won't stitch properly, most of the time it's because it isn't properly threaded up. Don't miss out any steps.

TIPS ON THREADING THE NEEDLE

1. RAISE the NEEDLE up to its HIGHEST POSITION.
2. Using sharp scissors, CUT the END of the SEWING THREAD. Tiny fibres are tightly wound together to form the thread. If you break the thread rather than cut it, the fibres spring apart at the end and make threading up difficult.
3. HOLD the SEWING THREAD between your FOREFINGER and THUMB so only a tiny amount of thread is visible. The rest should pass underneath your fingers.
4. LINE UP and PUSH the END of the SEWING THREAD through the EYE of the NEEDLE. Once it's through, pull the thread with your left hand. Put a finger through the loop on the right side until the thread is pulled all the way through. This will stop your thread from twisting around the needle.

BRINGING UP THE BOTTOM THREAD

1. RAISE the PRESSER FOOT. Make sure the MAIN SWITCH is turned OFF.
2. HOLD the top thread in your LEFT hand. With your right hand, TURN the HANDWHEEL (on the right side of your machine) TOWARDS you. Watch the needle go all the way down and then all the way back up to its HIGHEST position. Just once will do.
3. PULL the thread in your left hand sharply upwards. A loop should appear under the presser foot. That loop is the bottom thread coming from the bobbin. Grab it and pull it up until it's a single thread. Pull it long (about 10-12cm).
4. PASS both threads UNDER the PRESSER FOOT towards the back of the machine.

You're ready to go!

TENSION CONTROL

All sewing machines have a TENSION DIAL, which your sewing thread passes through. This dial controls the TIGHTNESS of the STITCHES. It's important that the dial is at the correct setting because you don't want your seams to pull apart. I usually have my dial set somewhere between 4 and 5. Sew a TEST SEAM. Pull the two fabric layers apart and look at your stitching. Is it too loose? Is it too tight? If it is either TOO LOOSE or TOO TIGHT, turn the tension dial a VERY TINY AMOUNT and test again. Repeat until the stitching looks good and the seams aren't loose.

WHICH MACHINE NEEDLE SHOULD I USE?

You MUST use the CORRECT NEEDLE for your choice of FABRIC, especially when sewing stretch fabrics. If you use an incorrect needle, then your sewing machine may SKIP STITCHES. If it does, you will end up with holes in your seams. Machine needles come in little packs of assorted sizes that you can buy at your local haberdashery or online. CHANGE your machine NEEDLE before each new project. A BLUNT needle can DAMAGE your fabric and cause missed stitches.

CHANGING THE NEEDLE

1. TURN OFF the sewing machine at the MAIN SWITCH.
2. LOWER the presser foot and turn the handwheel towards you to move the needle up to its highest position.
3. There will be a little screw somewhere close to the top of the needle shaft. UNDO this screw and pull out the old needle.
4. Take your new needle. You will see that the SHAFT at the top is FLAT on one side. This must be facing the BACK when the new needle is inserted into the machine.
5. With the NEW NEEDLE in the CORRECT POSITION, push it into the hole as far as it will go and TIGHTEN the SCREW.

MACHINE NEEDLE GUIDE

For woven (non-stretch) fabrics use UNIVERSAL NEEDLES in the following sizes:
Size 60/8 needles for very fine, lightweight fabrics, like silks.
Size 70/10 needles for lightweight cottons, voiles and polyesters.
Size 80/12 needle for medium-weight wovens, like cottons and chambrays.
Size 90/14 needles for heavy-weight wovens, like denims, canvas and corduroys.

For stretch jersey fabrics with a two-way stretch (from side-to-side) and most knitted fabrics, like cotton jersey, fleece, sweatshirt, Ponte di Roma and double knit, use BALLPOINT NEEDLES in the following sizes:
Size 70/10 ballpoint needles for lightweight fabrics
Size 80/12 ballpoint needles for medium- to heavyweight fabrics

For stretch jersey fabrics with a four-way stretch (side-to-side and up-and-down) like Lycra blends, spandex and elastane, use STRETCH NEEDLES in the following sizes:
Size 75/11 stretch needles for lightweight fabrics
Size 90/14 stretch needles for medium- to heavyweight fabrics

Size 120/20 needles are for very heavy fabrics and leather. I usually only buy needles in a size 70/10, 80/12 and 90/14 as these are for light- to mediumweight fabrics.

SEWING MACHINE BASICS

If you're completely new to machine sewing, then it's important to do some practise work first. If your sewing machine has a 'slow speed' option, select this before you start.

○ Make sure your sewing machine is correctly threaded up as per the manual.

○ Select a regular straight stitch.

○ Sit in a comfortable position. Your body should be directly in front of the needle. Your right foot must reach the peddle with your heel on the floor and toes pressing the peddle.

○ Make sure you have plenty of light. Your sewing machine should have a small light above the needle. This comes on when you turn on your machine.

○ When finishing a row of stitching, always pull the top and bottom threads nice and long. Do this every time you finish a row of stitching. If you leave your threads very short, then your machine will come unthreaded every time you start stitching your next row and you will waste a lot of time rethreading.

1

Place a strip of masking tape on base plate.

2

The masking tape acts as a guide to keep stitch lines straight.

3

Fold a piece of woven fabric together and pin raw edges.

4 Line up fabric raw edge to edge of the tape.

5 For straight stitches, keep fabric and tape aligned as you sew.

SEWING IN A STRAIGHT LINE

1 At first you may have trouble keeping your seams straight and parallel to the raw edges of the fabric. If this is the case, do as we do at The Fashion Factory - take some masking or electrical tape and place it on the base plate of the sewing machine so that you can use the edge of the tape as a guide for your fabric and keep the seam allowances the correct width. For our projects, we use a 1cm or 1.5cm seam allowance.

2 There are lots of little lines and measurements already on the base plate to act as guides. Place your tape on the 1cm or 1.5cm line. Line up the raw edge of your fabric with the edge of the tape at all times.

3 Take a piece of woven fabric and fold it in half. Pin together the raw edges (note the direction of the pins).

4 Line up the raw fabric edge to the strip of masking tape. Lower the presser foot. Practise sewing slowly to begin with until you feel comfortable and in control.

5 Keep practising. When sewing in straight lines, don't watch the needle. Instead watch the fabric edge and the tape. You will find that you become more accurate. When you are more confident, you can speed up.

FASHION FACT

SEAM ALLOWANCE:
The area of fabric between the LINE OF STITCHING and the RAW EDGE of the fabric is called the SEAM ALLOWANCE.

Backstitching is important when making clothes. If you don't backstitch at the beginning and end of every line of stitches, your seams will come undone as you wear your garment. Embarrassing! To backstitch, you need to find the reverse button or lever on your sewing machine. When you push or hold down this lever while sewing, the machine automatically sews backwards.

1 Reverse stitch to edge of fabric.

2 At end of seam, move take-up lever to its highest position.

3 Lift presser foot, pull out fabric and cut threads long.

Important!
Don't try making anything until you've learnt how to do this!

BACKSTITCHING A SEAM

1 On every seam, start about 1–1.5cm FORWARD of the raw edge. Hold down the reverse lever and slowly sew backwards until you reach the edge of your fabric. Stop. Let go of the reverse lever. Now start stitching your seam. That's your backstitching complete at one end.

2 Continue sewing your seam to the other end of the fabric. When you reach the very end, stop. Hold down the reverse lever and sew four or five stitches in reverse. Stop. Let go of the reverse lever. Stitch to the end of the seam. To remove your fabric from the machine, turn the handwheel manually towards you until the take-up lever (the lever on the very top of the machine that the thread passes through) is in its highest position.

3 Lift the presser foot. Pull the fabric out of the sewing machine and cut the threads, leaving them long. Now you have learnt how to backstitch, so you can make and wear garments knowing that your seams won't come undone.

1 Stop before corner, with your needle through fabric.

2 Lift presser foot, twizzle fabric to change direction.

3

When sewing seams you may sometimes need to turn a corner. To do this, you need to pivot. Just like in netball when one foot is fixed to the floor and you twizzle on the other, in sewing you lower the needle through the fabric, which acts as an anchor, so you can then twizzle the fabric in any direction.

SEWING ROUND A CORNER (PIVOTING)

1. Stop your line of stitching just before the corner. Turn the handwheel of your sewing machine (found on the right side) slowly towards you until you reach the turning point, with your sewing needle down through the fabric.
2. Lift the presser foot but leave the needle through the fabric. You can now pivot the fabric to change the direction of your sewing. Twizzle your fabric round until you are facing the right direction for the next line of stitching.
3. Lower the presser foot and continue sewing.

FINISHING RAW EDGES (WOVEN FABRICS ONLY)

When you cut out a garment in a woven fabric, you'll notice that the raw edges fray. This means that the fabric starts to unravel along the cut edges. If you make a piece of clothing but don't stop the raw edges from fraying, the fabric will fray more and more during wearing and washing and eventually the seams may come undone. In order to stop this, work a row of zigzag stitches along the EDGE of the seam allowance. Set your machine to a medium or large zigzag stitch, backstitch and sew a line of zigzag stitches along the raw edge of the fabric. Now your seams will be safe from bursting.

A dart transforms a flat piece of fabric into a three-dimensional shape, creating space for your bust. We do this by pinching out a triangle of fabric on both side seams, just below the armhole. If you look at the front bodice pattern for pattern B on the pattern sheet that accompanies this book, you'll see the bust darts marked on all sizes apart from size 1. Create your bust darts like this...

1 Mark bust dart side notches on your fabric with tailor's chalk.

2 Using a pin and tailor's chalk, mark bust point on your fabric.

3 Draw straight lines from marked side notches to bust point.

MARKING OUT A BUST DART

1 **LAY** your **BODICE PATTERN PIECE** on the **REVERSE SIDE** of your fabric and **MARK** the **SIDE NOTCHES** with tailor's chalk or very tiny snips in the seam allowance.

2 Using a pin, make a tiny hole in the paper pattern at the apex of the bust point. Using tailor's chalk, mark through the hole onto the fabric. If your fabric is patterned or your chalk doesn't show, carefully push the entire pin through the paper pattern to mark the position of the bust point on the fabric.

3 Using tailor's chalk and a ruler, **DRAW** straight lines to **JOIN UP** each of the **SIDE NOTCHES** with the **BUST POINT**.

4

Pinch together triangular bust dart, matching notches, and pin.

Sew from side seam to bust point.

5

Repeat and press bust dart downwards, towards hem.

6

PINNING AND SEWING A BUST DART

4 PINCH together the triangular BUST DART, matching up the side notches and pin along the marked lines. Note the direction of the pins.

5 Select a straight stitch on your machine. SEW from the SIDE SEAM towards the BUST POINT. BACKSTITCH at the start of the seam ONLY and then sew STRAIGHT OFF the end of the bust dart. Do NOT backstitch at the end. Leave the threads long at the end once you've finished sewing. Double knot the end threads and trim back to 1cm. This stops the bust dart from coming undone.

6 REPEAT at the other side seam to make a matching bust dart. Once sewn, STEAM PRESS the bust darts downwards, towards the hem.

FASHION FACT

NOTCHES are marker points on the fabric and are used for lining up key points. To make a notch, I usually make a small mark with tailor's chalk or make a tiny snip into the edge of the fabric. The snip should be no bigger than 2–3mm – just big enough to see. If you make the snips too big, then you'll be cutting into the garment. Use notches to line up waistbands with side seams or sleeveheads with shoulder seams.

When encountering a problem during sewing, ninety-nine times out of a hundred it's because the sewing machine is not properly threaded up. Sewing machines are precision instruments and have to be threaded up absolutely perfectly in order to sew correctly. The first thing to do is to check the manual that accompanies your sewing machine and rethread the machine according to those instructions, then, if it still won't sew, do this:

WHAT TO DO IF THERE'S A PROBLEM...

1. Check that your sewing machine is properly plugged in and correctly switched on.
2. Check that the handwheel is pushed in (or tightened). If you've just wound a bobbin, then the handwheel may still be disengaged.
3. Check that the thread on the bobbin is tightly wound and that the bobbin itself is correctly inserted. If you are using a top-loading sewing machine, when you look at the bobbin the thread should be coming from the left side of it when you put it into place (see page 27).
4. Check that you are using the correct type and size of machine needle for your chosen fabric (see page 29).
5. Has your sewing machine been recently cleaned? Machines can easily clog up with bits of fluff. Unplug the machine and follow the cleaning instructions given in your manual. Remember to clean the sewing machine under the base plate, too.
6. If all of the above checkpoints fail, then take your sewing machine to the local repair shop for a service.

YOUR FASHION JOURNEY STARTS HERE

THE
PROJECTS

LATEST LOGO T-SHIRT

Logos are a hot look and a firm favourite at The Fashion Factory. You can use letters, words, numbers or shapes for your logo and apply them to an old T-shirt, a loose-fitting top or even a simple T-shirt dress. You'll find a selection of templates for logos on the pattern sheet that comes with this book, which can be traced off or enlarged on a photocopier, or you can do your own thing. For complete beginners, shapes with straight edges are easier to sew round, so keep your logo simple. Remember that each shape must be individually cut from fabric, so bear this in mind when working out your design.

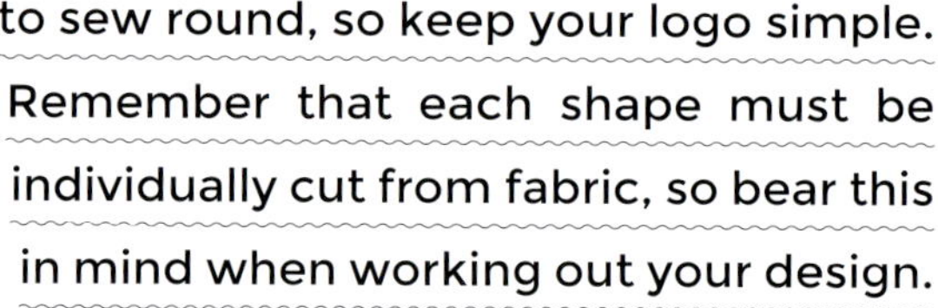

Take inspiration from the latest trends in books, magazines or photographs. You could choose a current typeface and enlarge it on a photocopier. Animal and insect logos are always popular. Once you've drawn out your logo, pick some really cool fabrics. You only need a little of each for a logo, so you could cut up and re-use things you already own.

APPLIQUÉ METHOD

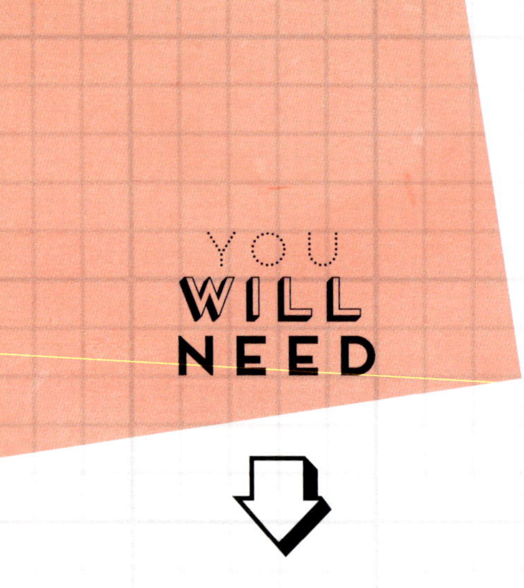

- Drawing paper
- Large T-shirt or top (choose one that is loose fitting, as it will be slightly smaller once it's finished)
- Sewing thread to match fabric
- Sewing thread for logo
- Selection of fabric scraps for logo
- Fusible bonding web (Bondaweb)
- Universal needle for your sewing machine
- Essential sewing equipment (see pages 12–13)

★★★★★★★★★★★★★★★★★★★★★

SETTING UP YOUR MACHINE

FIT a new UNIVERSAL NEEDLE in your sewing machine.

FASHION FACT

The RIGHT SIDE of a fabric is the side that will be on the OUTSIDE of the finished garment.

PREPARING YOUR T-SHIRT

PLACE your T-SHIRT on an IRONING BOARD. Using a hot iron, STEAM PRESS the top so it's completely FLAT and there are SHARP CREASES at the SIDE SEAMS and UNDERARM SEAMS.

Some T-shirts have side seams and some do not. If your T-shirt does NOT have side seams, PRESS in a CREASE where the seams would naturally be.

If you'd like your T-shirt to be SHORTER, carefully CUT it to the LENGTH you want. USE a MEASURING TAPE to make sure that the sides are EQUAL LENGTH and the bottom hem is not wonky.

1 Cut T-shirt open along side seams or side creases.

Cut underarm seams open and lay T-shirt out flat.

1 Carefully CUT your T-shirt OPEN along the SIDE SEAMS or SIDE CREASES. Cut EXACTLY along the seams. TRIM away any SEAM ALLOWANCE so that the EDGES are STRAIGHT and SMOOTH.

2 CUT right along the UNDERARM SEAMS, too, so that you can completely OPEN OUT your T-shirt FLAT. Now you can work on the FRONT PANEL without the back of the T-shirt getting in the way.

1 Draw out your design.

2 Trace each section of your design onto fusible bonding web.

3 Fuse bonding web shapes to fabric pieces.

DRAWING OUT YOUR DESIGN

1 DRAW out your chosen DESIGN (either your own or from the templates provided). THINK ABOUT the size of the motif (make sure it does NOT reach the side seams) as well as its shape and colour. When you place it on your garment, make sure you don't put it right on the edge in case it ends up disappearing into a seam. Place it no closer than 5-6cm to any edge. Once the logo is ready, decide whether your design needs to be reversed (see page 48). This is especially important if you're using letters or numbers.

ADDING YOUR DESIGN

2 Take a sheet of fusible bonding web and place it SHINY SIDE DOWN (glue side) on top of your design. TRACE off each SEPARATE SECTION of your logo. Do not waste your bonding web, so start in a corner rather than the middle and draw your shapes 1-2CM APART. Using paper scissors, roughly CUT OUT your shapes a tiny bit BIGGER all the way round.

3 Take your FABRIC SCRAPS and place them RIGHT SIDE DOWN on the ironing board. PLACE the cut-out bonding web shapes SHINY SIDE DOWN (glue side) on top of the scraps. PLACE a medium-hot IRON on top and HOLD until the GLUE has MELTED and the shape is completely FIXED onto the fabric round all the edges.

TIP

You'll need to buy some fusible bonding web – or Bondaweb – either at your local haberdashery or online. Fusible bonding web is like paper but has glue on the back, which is transferred onto the fabric using a hot iron. Ask someone to show you how to use your iron safely before you start sewing.

4

Carefully cut out logo shapes.

5 Peel off backing paper to prepare shapes for applying.

6 Permanently fix shapes and add definition with coloured stitching.

TIP

If you accidentally get glue on the hotplate of your iron, let it COOL DOWN before you attempt to get it off. Once the iron is cold, UNPLUG IT. Then you can use some VINEGAR or BAKING SODA mixed with a little water on an old CLOTH or TOOTHBRUSH. Rub hard!

4 Now carefully CUT OUT the logo shapes along the drawn outlines.

5 PEEL OFF the backing papers. You should see the glue is now attached to the back of the fabric shapes. If it is not, then press again with a hot iron until it is fixed.

ADDING YOUR DESIGN TO THE T-SHIRT

PLACE your logo shapes SHINY SIDE DOWN (glue side) on your T-shirt. Carefully line them up, noting the position of the CENTRE FRONT. Do not put your shapes too close to the side seams. Once in position, PLACE a medium hot IRON on top and HOLD until the GLUE has MELTED and the shape is completely FIXED in place.

6 Now FIX the logo shapes PERMANENTLY to your T-shirt and ADD some COLOUR and DEFINITION to the EDGES. This method of laying one piece of fabric on top of another and fixing in place is called APPLIQUÉ. Choose an embroidery stitch to sew round the edges of your design. Go to page 150 where there are some examples of simple machine embroidery stitches. Once your design is securely stitched in place, give it a good STEAM PRESS. Now is the time to add any extra details, like hand-stitching, buttons or trims.

Remove sleeve hems.

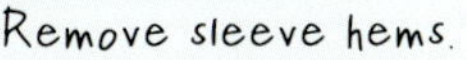

Pin together side and sleeve seams.

Stitch side and underarm seams, then trim seam allowance.

SEWING THE SIDE SEAMS AND SLEEVE SEAMS

7 Carefully REMOVE the hems of each sleeve.

8 TURN your T-shirt INSIDE OUT. PIN the side seams and underarm seams together as shown. Make sure you match up the armhole seams FRONT and BACK FIRST. Then PIN the ENDS together. Then PIN the rest of the SEAM from the SLEEVE EDGE to the HEM. If you'd like to make your T-shirt more fitted, then this is the time to do it. Don't take in too much at once - it's best to do it a little at a time.

9 Set your sewing machine to a STRAIGHT STRETCH STITCH or very small ZIGZAG STITCH. SEW your seam. BACKSTITCH at each end. REPEAT for the second SIDE SEAM. TRIM the seam allowances back to 1cm.

10 If you'd like TURN-BACKS on your SLEEVES, then make a DOUBLE FOLD at the sleeve ends. Hand or machine STITCH the double folds in place with a FEW STITCHES at the underarm seam.

10 For turn-backs, make a double fold and stitch in place.

APPLIQUÉ

ADDING LOGOS AND PICTURES TO CLOTHES

Appliqué (a French word pronounced app-lee-kay) is a way of adding decoration where one piece of cloth is fixed on top of another. It looks great and is a fun thing to do.

In order to do appliqué, you'll need to buy some fusible bonding web. This comes on a roll or in sheets; you can buy it at your local haberdashery or online. Fusible bonding web is paper on one side and glue on the other. By using a hot iron, you can transfer the glue from the fusible bonding web onto a fabric shape, or motif, so that it can be fixed onto a garment. Once the motif is in place, adding stitching around the edges will fix it permanently in place.

Using fusible bonding web – or Bondaweb – you can create any kind of motif, picture or logo. Keep your design simple to begin with. On the large sheet that accompanies this book, you will find a selection of motif templates. You can trace these off straight onto the paper side of the fusible bonding web, or enlarge them first on a photocopier, or you could draw up your own ideas. Whatever you do, remember that the shape has to be cut out in fabric.

You can use a wide range of fabrics for appliqué – cottons, silks, synthetics and stretch fabrics are all fine. However, avoid anything incredibly thick or bulky as it will be difficult to sew. And don't use a plastic- or nylon-based fabric, as it could melt onto your iron.

1

Make a reversed tracing of your chosen motif on paper.

2

Trace reversed motif onto fusible bonding web.

3

Roughly cut out motif in fusible bonding web.

Unless you REVERSE your APPLIQUÉ LOGO, it will come out back-to-front. If you don't want that to happen, especially if you are using LETTERS or NUMBERS, then you need to reverse the motif before transferring the outlines onto fusible bonding web.

REVERSING YOUR APPLIQUÉ MOTIF

1 To reverse your appliqué design, DRAW THE MOTIF onto plain paper. Using a window pane as a lightbox, tape this motif to the window with the drawn-on side against the glass so that the motif is in reverse. Using a marker pen, TRACE the shape onto the back of the paper so the OUTLINE IS NOW REVERSED. Put a MARK on this side, like a star or initials to remind you to use this side.

2 Place the SHINY SIDE (glue side) of the fusible bonding web ON TOP of your reversed design. TRACE it onto the PAPER SIDE.

3 CUT roughly round your shape, about 5mm away from the outline all the way round.

You're now ready to fuse the reversed motif onto your fabric scraps before cutting them out and applying them to your garment. Go back to step 3 on page 43 and continue making your appliqué.

4

COLOUR BLOCK SKATER SKIRT

LEVEL 1 PROJECT

This is a simple little skirt that can be made in hundreds of ways. In a stretch fabric, solid colour, printed or patterned to achieve both summer or winter versions. You could leave it completely plain or add some pretty tape, ribbon, lace or braid on top of your seams. The possibilities are almost endless. Without a zip or any buttons, it doesn't take long to make this skirt once you've prepared your paper pattern.

This skirt works very well in a medium- to heavyweight stretch fabric, such as Scuba jersey. It should have a good amount of stretch in it. I wouldn't recommend a fabric that is too lightweight, like a T-shirt jersey, as it could look a little drab and lifeless. This is a nice flippy skirt, so give it some bounce!

STRETCH FABRIC

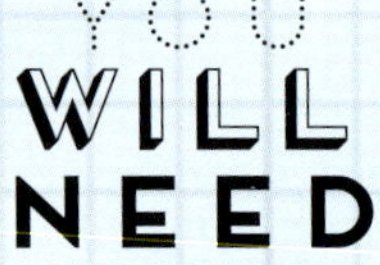

- Dressmaker's pattern paper
- Medium- or heavyweight stretch jersey fabric (use your paper pattern to work out how much fabric you need)
- Sewing thread to match fabrics
- Braid, ribbon or tape (optional)
- Ballpoint or stretch needle for sewing machine
- Essential sewing equipment (see pages 12–13)

MAKING YOUR PATTERN

For this project you need to use a SKIRT PATTERN that you make yourself. By creating your own pattern pieces, you can make a skirt that fits you perfectly. Do this before you buy your fabric – once you have the pattern pieces, you'll be able to work out exactly how much fabric you need. Go to page 20 to learn how to do this. Don't forget the waistband pattern as well.

BUYING YOUR FABRIC

This skirt works best in a medium- to heavyweight stretch jersey fabric, like a Ponte di Roma or Scuba jersey. Try to buy fabric that stretches mainly from side to side (two-way stretch). Unless you're a more experienced sewer, do NOT buy fabric that stretches from side to side AND up and down (four-way stretch), like many dance fabrics.

How much fabric you need will depend on the size of your paper pattern pieces. Once you've made the pattern, this is pretty easy to work out. If you're making this skirt in two colours, then you'll need to cut two panels in each colour. Most stretch fabrics are 150cm wide, so 0.5–0.75m of each fabric will be enough for most skirts, but make sure there's enough fabric for your waistband, too.

CHOOSING YOUR TRIMS

This skirt can be completely plain, or colour blocked, but you could also add some ribbon, braid, lace or tape to make it unique. It's best to apply it in straight lines over your seams. This can be done at the centre front, centre back, or at the sides. Choose something to go with your design, maybe a colour that you could match up with your shoes or accessories. White stripes will give a more sporty look. You could use lace or vintage ribbons if you'd like a pretty look. Brights could give a more retro look. Think about the latest trends for inspiration. Measure your seams and, using your measuring tape, work out how much you need.

CUTTING OUT THE SKIRT PANELS

You'll see that your fabric has two cut ends and two sides that look different. These finished sides that run up and down the length of the fabric are called SELVEDGES. This is where the fabric was fixed onto the machine that knitted it. It's important to identify and know where your selvedge is before you start pinning down your paper pattern piece and cutting out a garment.

When cutting out the skirt panels, ALWAYS PLACE THE CENTRE LINE PARALLEL TO THE SELVEDGES. This is important because the stretch runs across the fabric from selvedge to selvedge. Your skirt needs to do the same thing, so that it stretches out sideways when you pull it on, over your hips.

To make a four-panel skirt, you'll need to place the paper pattern close to the folded fabric edge, as shown. Pin and neatly cut out.

Using tailor's chalk, mark the CENTRE EDGE of each fabric panel; this helps you to match up the CENTRE seams at the FRONT and BACK.

Don't forget the waistband. This must be placed across the stretch fabric as well.

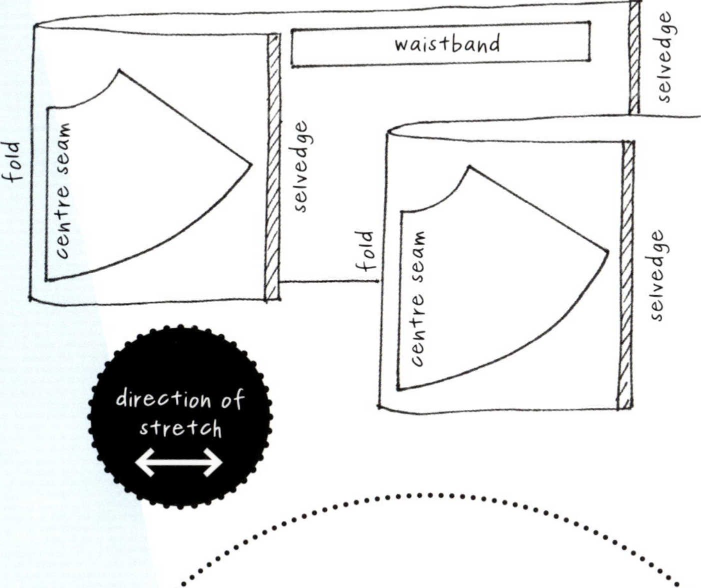

TIP

Use a STRAIGHT STRETCH STITCH (where the needle stitches two stitches forward and one stitch backwards). If your machine does NOT have a stretch stitch, then set it to a tiny ZIGZAG STITCH.

SETTING UP YOUR SEWING MACHINE

Fit a new BALLPOINT or STRETCH NEEDLE in your sewing machine. Make sure the flat part of the needle is facing the back.

Use a 1cm SEAM ALLOWANCE THROUGHOUT for this skirt. As a guide, PLACE a STRIP of TAPE along the 1cm line on the BASE PLATE and use this to LINE UP the RAW EDGE of the FABRIC.

If you haven't previously mastered this, PRACTISE sewing on a fabric scrap first. Do NOT stitch too fast. Take your time and become accurate before you speed up your sewing.

Cut out skirt panels and waistband. Mark centre edges with tailor's chalk.

1 Pin front skirt panels together along centre seam.

2 Stitch seam and then press seam allowances open.

3 Add your trim along length of centre seam.

TIP

Sew a test seam on a small cutting of fabric. Look at your stitching. Pull the seam apart. Does it look okay? Are the stitches too big? If so, change your stitch length or width dials until it looks right. Is the tension okay or are the stitches too loose? Check that your tension wheel is set to between 3 and 5.

MAKING THE SKIRT

1 LAY your two front skirt panels SIDE BY SIDE with RIGHT SIDES UP and CENTRE EDGES TOGETHER. FLIP the RIGHT PANEL ON TOP of the LEFT PANEL, using the CENTRE EDGES as your LINE OF SYMMETRY. They should now be RIGHT SIDES TOGETHER. PIN together along the CENTRE EDGE.

2 SET your sewing machine to a STRAIGHT STRETCH STITCH or a tiny ZIGZAG STITCH. (See notes on stitching stretch fabrics on page 24). Using a 1cm seam allowance, BACKSTITCH and then SEW the CENTRE SEAM from the WAIST at the top to the HEM at the bottom. BACKSTITCH at the end of the SEAM. STEAM PRESS the seam OPEN and FLAT. REPEAT steps 1 and 2 with the two back panels.

3 LAY the skirt panels RIGHT SIDE UP. Now you can ADD your TAPE, RIBBON, LACE or BRAID trim on top of your CENTRE FRONT SEAM. CUT it slightly LONGER than you need it. PIN it on from top to bottom. SEW down each side of the tape with a small ZIGZAG STITCH and in a MATCHING COLOUR to the ribbon (if you use a matching colour and wobble a bit, then it won't show up). Each time start at the top of the skirt, at the waist, and STITCH DOWNWARDS towards the hem. If it's a very narrow ribbon, then just one row of zigzag stitching down the centre is fine. If it's a lace

Sew together front and back skirt panels. 4

Fold waistband in half. Mark centre with a pin. 5

Pin waistband to centre front and side seams. 6

trim, then stitch down the straight edge. TAKE YOUR TIME and try to be NEAT because this is the FOCAL POINT of your design. When you're done, give it a good PRESS and TRIM away the excess at the WAIST EDGE only.

4 Now place the FRONT and BACK panels RIGHT SIDES TOGETHER. PIN together one side seam. Using a stretch stitch or small zigzag SEW your SIDE SEAM from the WAIST to the HEM. BACKSTITCH at each end. PRESS the seam open.

7 Add more pins all the way along waistband.

ADDING THE WAISTBAND

5 FOLD the waistband in half, RIGHT SIDE OUT. Find the CENTRE POINT and MARK it with a PIN.

6 With your skirt RIGHT SIDE UP, PLACE the RAW EDGES of the WAISTBAND ON TOP of the skirt WAISTLINE, with the FOLDED EDGE at the bottom. PIN the ENDS of the WAISTBAND to the ENDS of the SKIRT. PIN the CENTRE MARKER PIN to the stitched SIDE SEAM of the skirt.

7 Add LOTS OF PINS along the waistband in between. Take your time and make sure the waistband is STRETCHED and PINNED EVENLY onto the TOP EDGE of the skirt. (You might find it easier if you ask someone else to hold the ends and stretch the waistband while you do the pinning.)

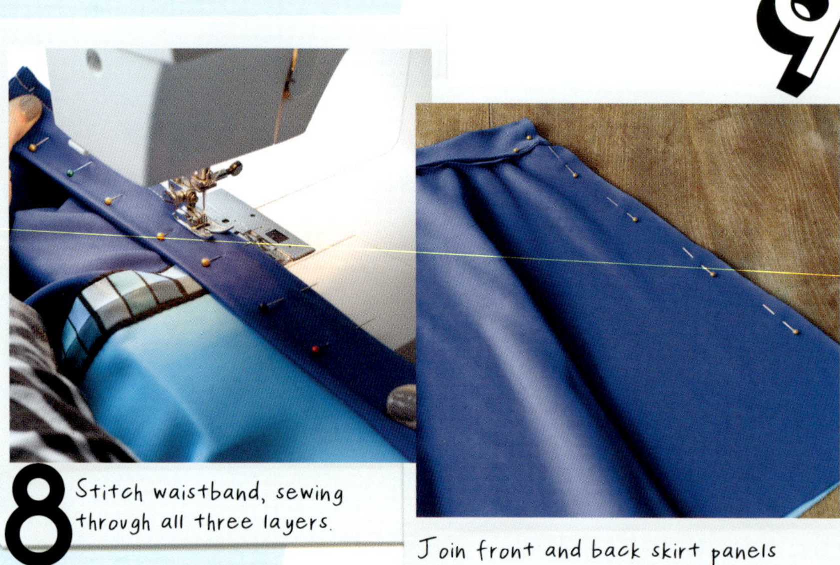

8 Stitch waistband, sewing through all three layers.

9 Join front and back skirt panels at the remaining side seam.

10 Turn end of ribbon or braid under and stitch.

8 Set your machine to a STRAIGHT STRETCH STITCH or a small ZIGZAG STITCH. Starting at the left side, slightly stretching the fabric in front and behind the needle as you sew, slowly sew over the pins. BACKSTITCH at both ends. Check at every pin that you're sewing through only three layers of fabric. Pleats can form under your sewing. Remove the pins.

9 FOLD your skirt in half with RIGHT SIDES TOGETHER. PIN from the waist to the hem. Sew with a 1cm seam allowance. BACKSTITCH. If you get STUCK on the WAISTBAND SEAM where there are lots of layers of fabric, try PULLING the fabric GENTLY from the BACK or MANUALLY TURNING your MACHINE HANDWHEEL TOWARDS YOU until it's sewn. If your machine MISSES a few STITCHES below the waistband, it's because of the change in FABRIC THICKNESS; just BACKSTITCH over the area until it's covered. Be AWARE of what your sewing machine is doing at this point.

With your skirt INSIDE OUT, STEAM PRESS the side seam OPEN and FLAT. Time to TRY ON your skirt. It should look fab! (If it's TOO BIG, you can RE-SEW your LAST SIDE SEAM by sewing again a little FURTHER AWAY from the edge. Try on again, then trim away your first seam.

HEMMING THE SKIRT

Now you need to decide how you want to finish the raw edge of your skirt at the hemline. Because it's a stretch fabric, it's not going to fray so you could leave the hem as a RAW EDGE. If you do, you'll need to make sure that it's EVENLY CUT all the way round, especially at the side seams where it should join perfectly.

10 TURN the END of your ribbon or braid under and neatly FIX inside with a few SMALL HAND STITCHES.

If you want a neat finish to your skirt, TURN UNDER 1cm of THE HEMLINE all the way round and PIN. Take care to keep it 1CM ALL THE WAY ROUND. Set your machine to a LARGE ZIGZAG STITCH and make sure your bobbin is full of a sewing thread in a colour to match your skirt fabric (as the stitching will show). For a very professional look, CHANGE THE BOBBIN COLOUR so that each panel is stitched with a MATCHING THREAD. Start at the CENTRE BACK seam, with the EDGE of the PRESSER FOOT to the EDGE of the FOLD. BACKSTITCH. SEW SLOWLY and, at the same time, GENTLY PULL as you sew. This helps to keep the HEM CURVED. BACKSTITCH at the end.

Your hem now needs a good STEAM PRESS to SHRINK back any STRETCHING that has occurred. Lay the skirt on the ironing board (don't let it stretch over the edges), HOLD the IRON very CLOSELY above the HEM and STEAM HEAVILY in sections. Take some time over this and you will see that all of the stretching will shrink. Finally, give the whole skirt a full press. TRIM away any loose threads.

When attaching the waistband, CHECK at EVERY PIN that you're SEWING through ONLY THREE LAYERS of fabric. Pleats can easily form under your sewing.

RIP IT UP!

ADDING FABRIC STRIPS

There are so many types of pretty lace, ribbon and tape around these days – adding these additional strips of fabric is a quick and easy way of adding a decorative element to your design. You can recycle by cutting trims off old clothing. I like to go to carboot sales and charity shops to search for trims to re-use, but online auction sites are also a great way of finding vintage ribbons and lace.

Rip up strips of fabric and lay them at angles across or alongside your seams. Pin them along the centres, then stitch them on with a zigzag or a fancy embroidery stitch. If you're using lace, it's best to stitch it on with a small zigzag stitch.

SHIRRED SHIRT DRESS

A quick and easy project that can be made from an old shirt. The shirt dress looks great worn with leggings or jeans during any season. Dad's old work shirt would do (ask him first) or you could upcycle a second-hand one. Look out for bright or ditsy floral prints, trendy checks, lightweight denim or chambray or gorgeous colours in charity shops or at a carboot sale. The shirt should be nice and roomy and fairly long on you. Look out for ones that have shirt tails (curved hemlines that shape upwards at the side seams).

In this project you will add shirring elastic (pronounced sheer-ring) to the waistline to give the dress its nipped in shape. Shirring is pretty easy to do once you know how and has many uses (waistlines, cuffs and even necklines). You could change the buttons and add nice tape or ribbon ties at the waistline. Use a shorter shirt for a tunic version.

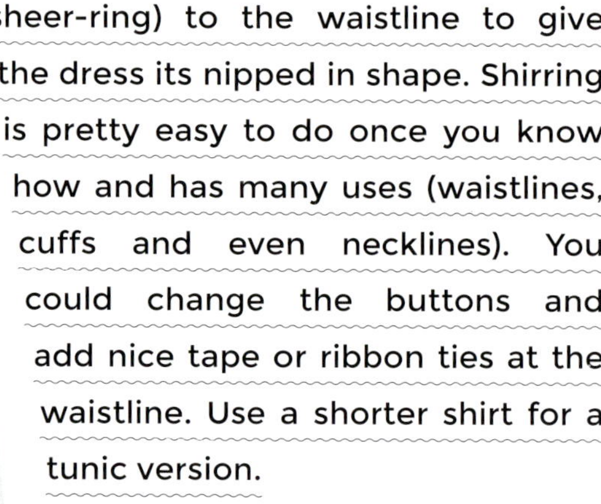

DAD'S SHIRT
UPCYCLED

YOU WILL NEED

- Old shirt (the chest measurement should be approximately 25–35cm larger than your own chest)
- Sewing thread to match shirt fabric
- Shirring elastic (like thread, but stretchy)
- 1m ribbon or tape, for front ties
- Buttons (optional)
- Universal needle for sewing machine
- Essential sewing equipment (see pages 12–13)

★★★★★★★★★★★★★★★★

PREPARING YOUR SHIRT

Some men's shirts have a breast pocket on one side. You can either leave this where it is or turn your shirt INSIDE OUT and, working from the BACK ONLY, use your seam ripper to CAREFULLY CUT all the stitches. It won't take long as it's only three rows of straight stitching. Once the pocket is removed completely, you might see a row of tiny holes where the stitches used to be. To get rid of these holes, gently RUB the SHARP END of a PIN over them. They should totally disappear, because you are moving the individual fibres of the fabric back into their original place.

SETTING UP YOUR MACHINE

FIT a new UNIVERSAL NEEDLE in your sewing machine.

Use a 1CM SEAM ALLOWANCE throughout for this shirt dress. As a guide, PLACE the RIGHT EDGE of the PRESSER FOOT on the RAW EDGE of the FABRIC or PLACE a STRIP of TAPE along the 1cm line on the BASE PLATE and use this to LINE UP the RAW EDGE of the FABRIC.

Always BACKSTITCH at the BEGINNING and END of every line of STITCHES.

1 Cut off your collar, but leaving collar stand.

2 Draw a line on shirt to mark your waistline.

3 Sew rows of shirring elastic.

MAKING THE SHIRT DRESS

1 Using sharp fabric scissors, carefully CUT OFF the SHIRT COLLAR. DO NOT CUT the COLLAR STAND (the part of the shirt that the collar is fixed to). REMOVE any LOOSE ENDS and THREADS so that it's neat. This will leave you with a 'granddad' style collar.

PUT the SHIRT ON and stand in front of a mirror. Your SHIRRING ELASTIC should run from a BUTTON on one side of the shirt to a BUTTONHOLE on the other side, either ON or CLOSE TO your NATURAL WAISTLINE. MARK the POSITION with a PIN.

2 LAY out your shirt RIGHT SIDE UP. Using tailor's chalk or a pencil and a ruler, DRAW A LINE all the way round your waistline FROM THE BUTTON on one side TO THE BUTTONHOLE on the other side. Make sure that the distance from the hemline to your drawn line measures the same at both side seams.

3 Undo the shirt buttons. Now ADD rows of SHIRRING ELASTIC to the waistline. GO TO PAGE 64 to learn how it's done. Make sure that you SEW ON TOP OF YOUR LINE FIRST. Start and finish as close to your button or buttonhole as possible. You'll need a MINIMUM of TWO ROWS of elastic.

DESIGN **IDEA**

If you'd like to dip dye, tie dye or add embroidery to your shirt, go to pages 67–9 to learn how to do this.

HOW TO: ADD SHIRRING ELASTIC

You can add shaping to a garment with shirring (pronounced sheer-ing). It's a pretty easy thing to do and always looks impressive. You will need some shirring elastic. This comes on a spool, like a roll of thread, but it's elastic instead. You can buy it easily online or at your haberdashers. It comes in various colours.

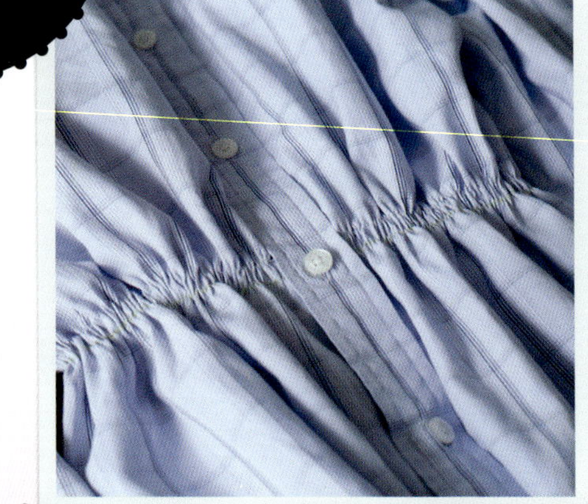

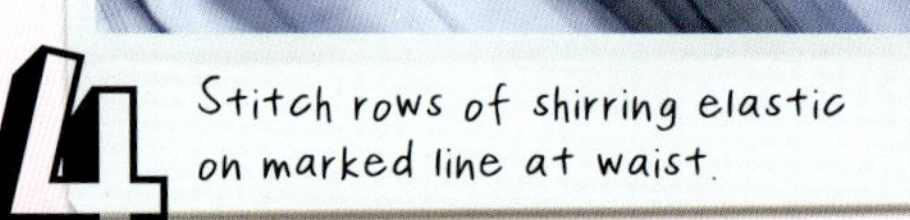

4 Stitch rows of shirring elastic on marked line at waist.

5 Cut off shirt cuffs above the placket opening.

ADDING SHIRRING ELASTIC

4 HAND WIND your BOBBIN with the ELASTIC until it's full. DO NOT STRETCH IT AS YOU GO. Thread up your machine in the normal way. Use a regular sewing thread on the top in a colour that matches your fabric; if the colour matches, then any wobbles won't show up.

Set your machine to a LARGE STRAIGHT STITCH. You will be stitching on the RIGHT SIDE of your garment, so make sure it's RIGHT SIDE UP when you're sewing. BACKSTITCH TWICE. Keeping the fabric flat, STITCH your first row on the marked line. BACKSTITCH TWICE at the end.

MOVE your shirt dress OVER SLIGHTLY so that the edge of the presser foot is against your first row of stitching. BACKSTITCH TWICE. Sew a second row of shirring. Gently PULL the FABRIC from both the FRONT and the BACK to keep it FLAT. Do NOT sew over pleats.

REPEAT this process until you have as many rows of shirring as you need. ALWAYS BACKSTITCH TWICE to stop the elastic from pinging back on itself when stretched. TRIM any THREADS on the REVERSE SIDE, leaving the shirring elastic approximately 2cm long.

6 Double fold the sleeve edges to the length required.

7 Stitch the underarm seam to hold the sleeve turnings in place.

8 Add folded ribbon details to both cuffs.

SEWING THE SLEEVES

5 LAY out your shirt dress and CUT OFF the CUFFS, just ABOVE the SLEEVE PLACKET (the opening above the cuff). Using a measuring tape, check both sleeves are EQUAL LENGTH.

6 FOLD BACK the SLEEVE EDGE and then BACK AGAIN to get the length you want. PIN in place and try on. Are they the correct length? If not, redo.

7 Remember to return to a BOBBIN filled with regular SEWING THREAD to sew the sleeves. Using a STRAIGHT STITCH, pin and sew the turning on the UNDERARM SEAM to hold your turning back.

8 Decide on your SLEEVE DETAIL. I used a very small piece of RIBBON, folded as shown. PIN in place and STITCH as shown.

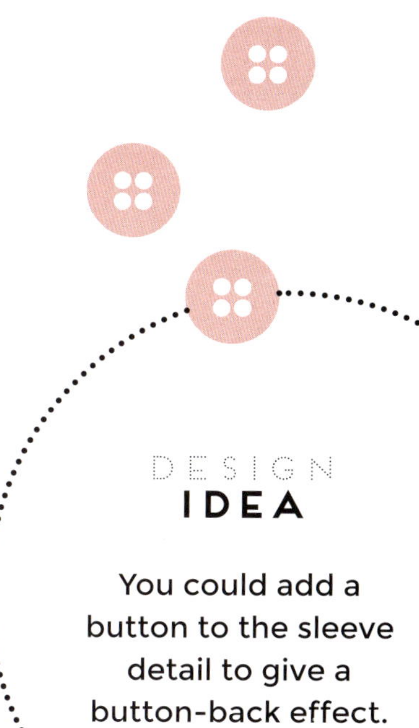

DESIGN **IDEA**

You could add a button to the sleeve detail to give a button-back effect.

9 Stitch lengths of ribbon on top of shirring facing towards sides.

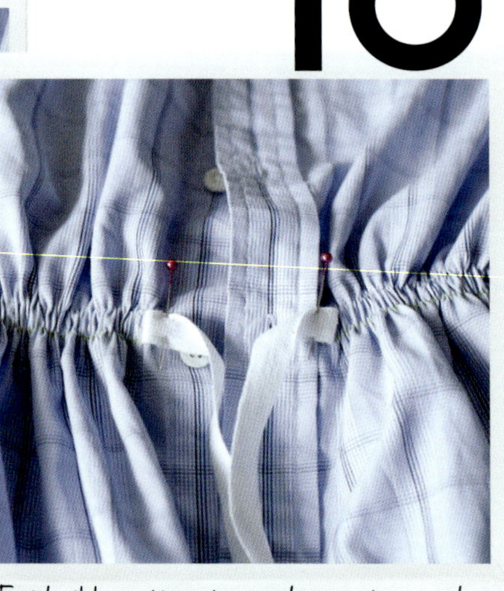

10 Fold ribbon ties towards centre and stitch ends again.

Tie ribbons in a bow at waist to add shaping.

12 Stitch bottom section closed if it's too long.

ADDING THE RIBBON TIES

9 Cut two LENGTHS OF RIBBON 35-40cm long and PIN them ON TOP of your SHIRRING, facing towards the sides. BACKSTITCH. STRAIGHT STITCH across the ribbons close to the ends.

10 FOLD the ribbons back the other way and STITCH AGAIN 5mm from the ends.

11 TIE the lengths of ribbon in a BOW at the waist to add shape to the shirt dress.

12 If your shirt dress is very long and flaps open below the waist when worn, you could STITCH the BOTTOM SECTION CLOSED. Use a matching thread and straight stitch on top of the placket. TRIM any loose threads and PRESS.

DIP DYE

Whether you're dip dying or tie dying fabric, your garment or fabric should be made primarily from a natural fibre, like cotton, silk or viscose (see the instructions for tie dye on pages 68–9). Prepare your dye bath in exactly the same way. If your garment or fabric is brand new, then wash and dry it first. Wear rubber gloves and an apron.

Prepare your dye bath following the instructions on page 69. Add plenty of salt. Holding the top (or shoulders), dip the whole garment, or most of it, just quickly to give a light base colour first. Then leave just the bottom of the garment in the dye for 3–5 minutes (hang it over the side of the bowl). Then dip a little more into the dye for another 3–5 minutes. Then repeat again. Adjust your timings to suit the depth of colour you require. Rinse in cold water. Hang up to dry. Wash separately by hand for the first few washes or until the dye no longer leaks out during washing.

DESIGN
IDEA

How about experimenting with old knitwear? Use knits that are cotton-rich.

TIE DYE

Tie dye is very effective and yet very easy to do. This is the easiest and quickest version of the technique. Your garment or fabric needs to be made of a natural fibre, like cotton, silk or viscose (made from tree bark). Maybe you have a top that is cotton and polyester. That's okay, but the colour may not come out as strong as it would on 100% cotton. It will still work, but it will be a slightly lighter shade. Make sure it's minimum 65% natural fibre.
If it's brand new, wash and dry it first.

When laundering any garment that has been tie dyed, wash it separately by hand for the first few washes or until the dye no longer leaks out.

If you want to add other colour, then make two or three dye baths and dip different parts of your tied garment separately into each bath. Experiment.

1

To make stripes, pleat garment and then tie at intervals.

2

To make spirals, twist garment into swirls and then tie.

3

Stretch lots of rubber bands over fabric or tie with string.

MAKING STRIPES

Walk your fingers across the fabric in tiny steps to create very small pleats or folds. Next, wrap the pleats and tie tightly with string (or use rubber bands). Leave a gap then repeat at regular intervals. Make sure you wrap and tie the fabric tightly. If it's not tight enough, you won't have any pattern on your garment, only colour.

MAKING SPIRALS

For large or small swirls, lay the garment flat and twist it tightly. Next, apply rubber bands or tie tightly with string.

PREPARING THE DYE BATH

Wear rubber gloves. Into a large bowl or bucket add some warm water, enough to cover completely your one item to be dyed. Add a large handful of salt and stir until it's dissolved. The salt helps the fibres to absorb the colour. Add your 50g pack of cold hand dye and stir well until it's completely dissolved.

Put your garment into the dye bath and leave it for at least 20 minutes, turning it regularly. Remove it from the dye and leave it to dry out on newspaper for at least an hour before snipping the ties. Rinse briefly in cold water. Hang it up to dry.

HOW TO PIMP YOUR DENIM

LEVEL 1 & 2 PROJECTS

There's sooooo much denim on this planet. So let's upcycle it! If you already have old denim jeans, use those. If not, buy some cheaply at a carboot sale or charity shop. Just make sure the jeans are clean and pressed before you start sewing. Why not have a go at making your own versions of these upcycled denim ideas?

FUNK UP YOUR SHORTS

LEVEL 1 PROJECT

This is a super-easy upcycling project that you can do very quickly. You'll need a pair of denim jeans (not too stretchy) and some lovely lace trim.

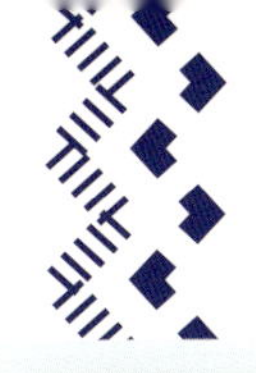

1 Mark required leg length of shorts on reverse side of denim.

2 Cut away legs along lines. Pin lace around bottom edge.

3 Stitch trim in place, securing ends at inside leg seam.

1 PUT your jeans on INSIDE OUT. MARK with a PIN the point on each leg where you want the shorts to finish.

TAKE your jeans off and LAY them out FLAT. Using tailor's chalk or a felt-tip pen and a ruler, DRAW a LINE across each leg at the marker pin. Using a measuring tape, check both legs are EQUAL LENGTH and that your lines are at RIGHT ANGLES to the SIDE SEAMS.

2 Using sharp fabric scissors, CUT along the LINES to REMOVE the lower LEGS and TURN the JEANS into SHORTS.

TURN the jeans RIGHT SIDE OUT. Take a length of lace or edge trim and, starting at the INSIDE LEG SEAM, PIN it to the HEM of the shorts all the way round. OVERLAP the ends of the trim by 1-2cm at the inside leg seam join.

3 REMOVE the accessory tray from your sewing machine to reveal the free arm. Set your machine to a medium-large ZIGZAG STITCH. SLIDE the JEAN LEG over the FREE ARM.

Starting at one inside leg seam, SEW along the TOP EDGE of the trim. When you get to the inside leg join, PIVOT and STITCH to close the trim ends. PRESS. REPEAT for the second leg.

DESIGN **IDEA**

How about using tassel fringing instead of lace trim for a festival vibe?

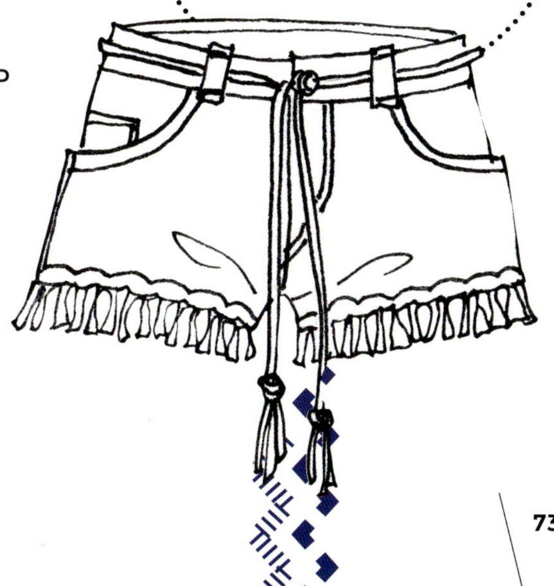

ADDING LACE TRIM

There are millions of different kinds of lace trim. If you buy a cotton lace, wash it before you attach it to your garment because it may shrink slightly when washed.

Pin lace trim to backing fabric, placing pins with care.

Stitch along top edge of lace trim, following straight or shaped top edge.

Trim away backing fabric to showcase lace.

ADDING STRAIGHT-EDGED LACE OR SHAPED-EDGE LACE

1 LAY out the FABRIC to which the lace is being applied with the RIGHT SIDE FACING UPWARDS. PLACE the LACE trim along the BOTTOM EDGE of the fabric and PIN at regular intervals, as shown.

2 Set your sewing machine to a small/medium ZIGZAG STITCH. Using thread in a colour to match the lace trim, SEW SLOWLY and carefully along the straight top edge or shaped top edge.

3 FLIP OVER the fabric and lace, and using sharp fabric scissors, TRIM away the backing fabric to within 1–2mm of the stitching.

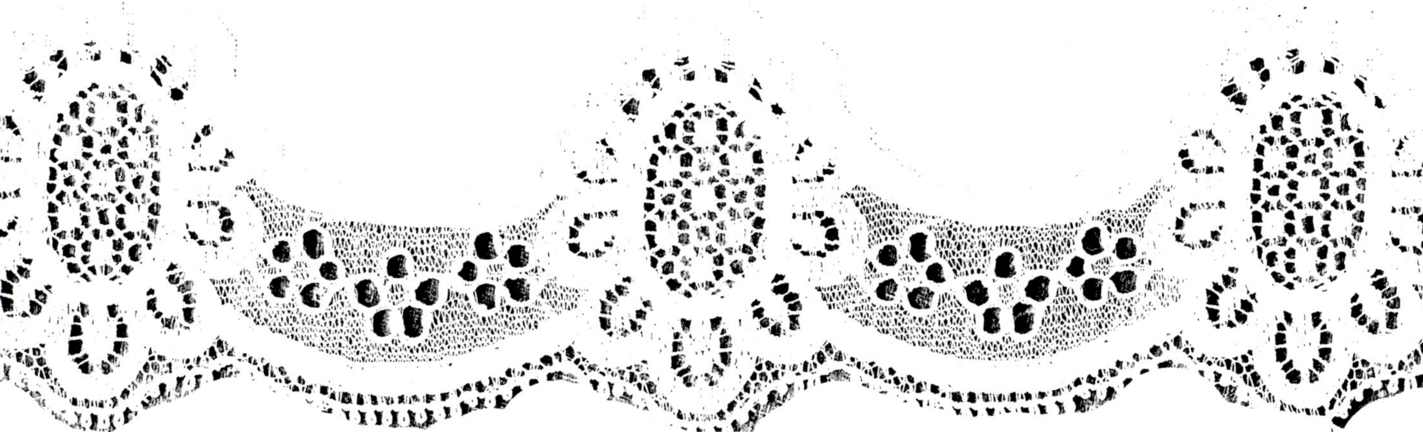

DENIM MINI SKIRT

LEVEL 2 PROJECT

This is an easy skirt to make from an old pair of jeans that may have become just a bit too small for you. Once they're made into a skirt, you'll find that they fit quite comfortably again. Either use denim throughout or choose a funky print to insert at the front and back joins. You could add some lace trim to the bottom edge afterwards, instead of turning under the hemline, or decorate with a selection of badges. This works best with jeans that are made with light- to medium-weight denim.

1 Mark required length of skirt on reverse side of legs.

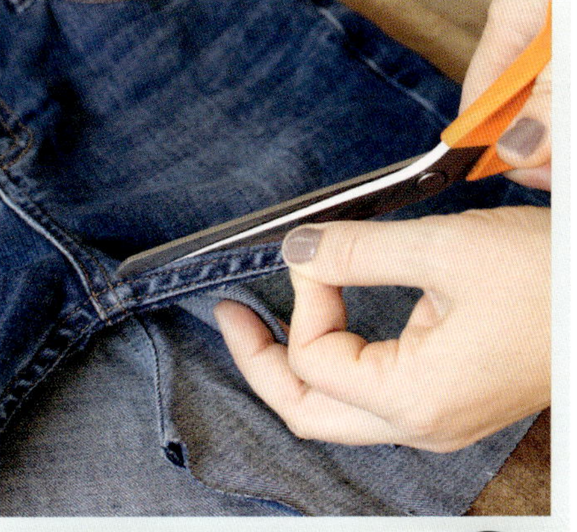

Trim away thick inside leg seams along front edge. 2

3 Cut upwards along front crotch, towards zip.

1 PUT your jeans on INSIDE OUT. MARK with a PIN the point on each leg where you want the skirt to finish.

TAKE your jeans off and LAY them out FLAT. PIN back the POCKET BAGS.

Using tailor's chalk or a fibre-tip pen and a ruler, DRAW a LINE across each leg 2cm BELOW the marker pin. Using a measuring tape, check both legs are EQUAL LENGTH and that your lines are at RIGHT ANGLES to the SIDE SEAMS.

Using sharp fabric scissors, CUT along the LINES to REMOVE the lower LEGS.

2 Turn the jeans RIGHT SIDE OUT and CUT OPEN along the inside leg SEAM. Do NOT cut along the outside leg seam. TRIM away the thick INSIDE LEG SEAM.

3 CUT upwards along the FRONT CROTCH SEAM to about HALF WAY UP. Do NOT cut right up to the base of the zip.

4 PULL the cut-open part of the front crotch seam ACROSS, from one side over to the other, so that it overlaps. PIN the seam so that it lies FLAT. REPEAT at the BACK CROTCH SEAM, cutting only the CURVED PART of the seam.

Pin overlapping crotch seam flat. Repeat at back. 4

5

Trim bottom edge of skirt across back to an equal length.

6

Turn under 1cm along raw front edges and press.

7

Place patch inside skirt to fill gap. Stitch. Repeat at back.

5 Using sharp fabric scissors, TRIM the BOTTOM EDGE of the skirt across the BACK to an EQUAL LENGTH.

6 TURN UNDER 1cm along both raw front edges. PRESS.

7 CUT out a small PATCH of denim from one of the discarded legs. Place the patch INSIDE your skirt to fill the gap in the FRONT CROTCH SEAM, with the RIGHT SIDE UPWARDS. Make sure that the fabric is ON GRAIN and reaches up as far as the ZIP inside the skirt.

Using a thread to match the colour of the jeans topstitching, PIN and STITCH along the turned-under edges. REPEAT at the back crotch seam.

LEVEL the HEM, then turn your skirt inside out and TRIM away any excess denim from the patch. PRESS. Stitch just above the hem line with large ZIGZAG STITCHES in either a matching or contrast thread.

DESIGN
IDEA

Instead of denim, you could add a patch of printed fabric at the front. How about adding freestyle 'doodle' embroidery, stitching on some badges or attaching a length of lace trim or fringing?

HAND PAINTING

Hand painting looks great on fabric, especially denim. You can buy textile paints easily online. It's best to plan out your design first on paper, then copy it onto your garment with a pen or pencil. Don't put the paint on too thickly, as it may crack and peel off during washing. You must heat seal the paint when it's dry. Use a hot iron on the reverse side of the fabric. Always cool wash a hand-painted garment separately for the first few washes.

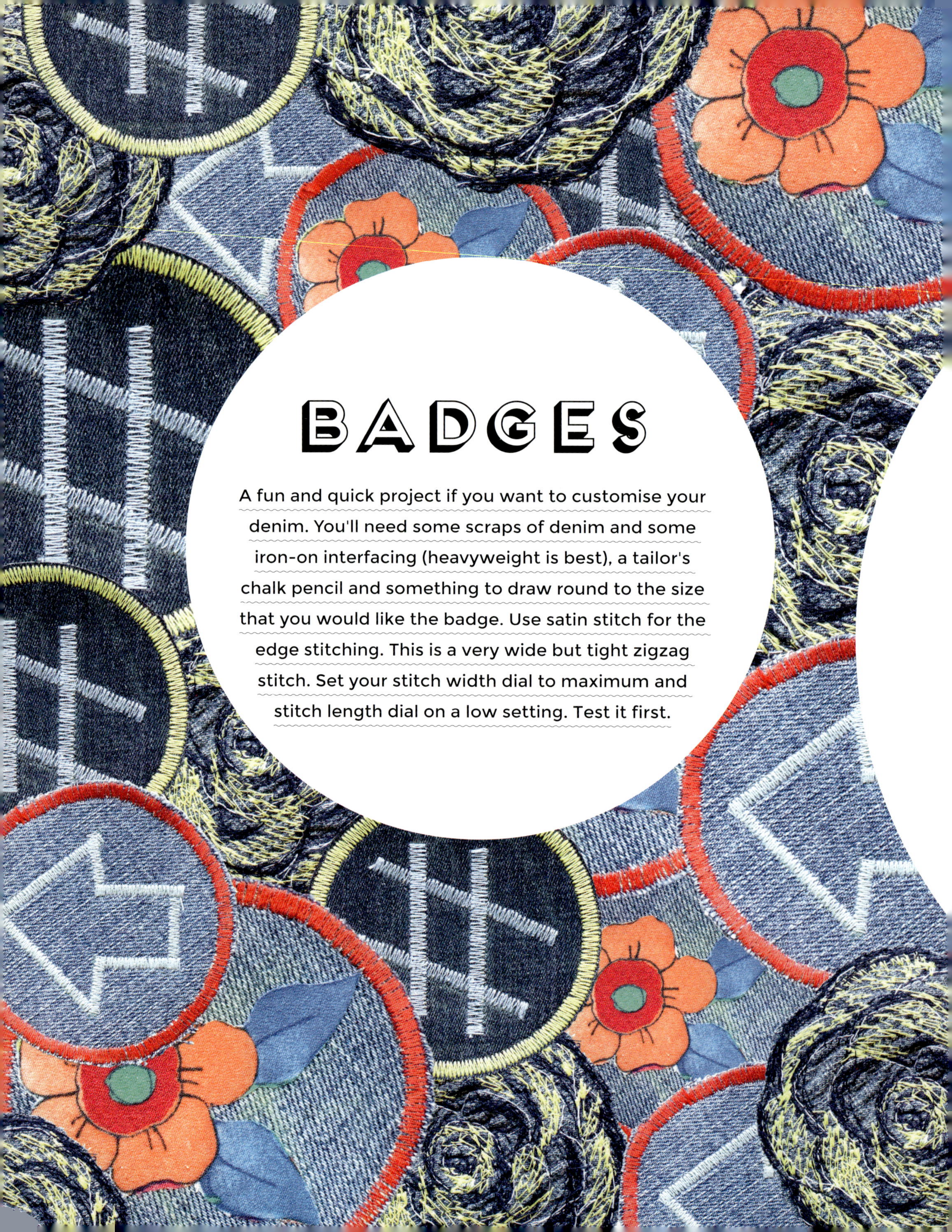

BADGES

A fun and quick project if you want to customise your denim. You'll need some scraps of denim and some iron-on interfacing (heavyweight is best), a tailor's chalk pencil and something to draw round to the size that you would like the badge. Use satin stitch for the edge stitching. This is a very wide but tight zigzag stitch. Set your stitch width dial to maximum and stitch length dial on a low setting. Test it first.

1 Draw your badge design on a scrap of denim or other fabric.

2 Apply the iron-on interfacing to the reverse of the fabric.

3 Using a wide satin stitch, work over the drawn outlines.

(1) With your fabric RIGHT SIDE UPWARDS, DRAW the circular OUTLINE for the badge. A circle approximately 7–8cm in diameter is a good size. Next, DRAW your DESIGN in the CENTRE of the circular OUTLINE.

(2) FLIP the fabric over and, on the REVERSE SIDE, ADD the iron-on INTERFACING, glue side down. Completely cover the area to be used for the badge. I prefer to use TWO LAYERS of a heavyweight interfacing. Alternatively, you could use several layers of a lightweight interfacing.

(3) Set your sewing machine to a wide SATIN STITCH. SEW slowly along the circular OUTLINE. Keep the centre channel of the presser foot on top of the drawn outline at all times. Once the outline is stitched, SEW the DESIGN. You may want to alter the stitch width or completely change the style of stitch.

Once all the stitching is done, trim away the excess fabric to leave a nice round badge. Hand stitch the finished badge onto your jeans, skirt or jacket.

RETRO
JEANS
BAG
LEVEL 2 PROJECT

This is such a cute bag that can be made in loads of different ways - large or small, depending on the size of your jeans. Start your own bag trend: make one for yourself and then lots of different versions for your friends. You need some old denim jeans and a tie or belt or strip of printed fabric. How about adding badges or your own logos and doodles to customise your bag (go to pages 43-4 and 80-81).

1 TURN your jeans INSIDE OUT and CUT across the legs, approximately 5-10cm below the crotch seam. Using a measuring tape, check both legs are EQUAL LENGTH and that your CUTS are at RIGHT ANGLES to the SIDE SEAMS.

1 Cut across the legs 5-10cm below crotch seam.

2 Trim away thick inside leg seams along front edge.

3 Pull cut-open part of front crotch seam across.

2 Using sharp fabric scissors, CUT OPEN along the inside leg SEAM. Do NOT cut along the outside leg seam. CUT upwards along the FRONT CROTCH SEAM to about half way up. Do NOT cut right up to the base of the zip. TRIM away the thick INSIDE LEG SEAM.

3 PULL the cut-open part of the front crotch seam ACROSS, from one side over to the other, so that it overlaps. PIN the seam so that it lies FLAT. REPEAT at the BACK CROTCH SEAM, cutting only the CURVED PART of the seam.

4 Trim bottom edge of bag across back to an equal length.

5 Trim away any excess fabric from patch.

6 Pin and stitch bottom edges together and finish with a zigzag.

If you want to add any embroidery or logos to your bag panels, now is the time to do it.

4 CUT out a PATCH of denim from one of the discarded legs. Place the patch INSIDE your skirt to fill the gap in the FRONT CROTCH SEAM, with the RIGHT SIDE UPWARDS. Make sure that the fabric is ON GRAIN and reaches up as far as the ZIP inside the skirt.

Using a thread to match the colour of the denim, SEW a line of large ZIGZAG STITCHES on the raw front edges almost as far as the zip. (I use a heavy double zigzag stitch.) REPEAT at the back crotch seam.

PIN the front and back waist edges together and, using sharp fabric scissors, LEVEL the bottom edge of the bag across the back to an EQUAL LENGTH to match the front.

5 TURN your bag INSIDE OUT and TRIM away any excess fabric from the denim patch. PRESS.

6 PIN the front and back bottom edges together. Set your sewing machine to STRAIGHT STITCH and, leaving a 1.5cm seam allowance, stitch along the bottom edge. Then work a line of large ZIGZAG STITCHES to stop any fraying.

TURN the bag the RIGHT SIDE OUT. PUSH out the CORNERS.

7 Cut a long shoulder strap from spare denim.

Turn under 1cm, press and stitch along both long edges.

Pin straps in place around waist, then stitch securely. 9

MAKING AND ATTACHING THE SHOULDER STRAP

7 From the discarded denim, CUT out a long SHOULDER STRAP. If your denim isn't big enough, CUT TWO EQUAL LENGTHS and STITCH them together in the CENTRE. For the width, cut the strap 2cm wider than you need.

8 TURN UNDER 1cm along both LONG EDGES and PRESS. Pin and then ZIGZAG STITCH these turnings in place, or use an embroidery stitch, if you prefer.

9 PLACE your shoulder strap ends INSIDE the waistband on each side of the bag, then PIN in place. STITCH the strap ends to the waistband. If your sewing machine struggles to sew across the belt loops, work a square or rectangle of stitches each side of the belt loop.

10 To close the bag's top edge, add small pieces of Velcro fastening tape (sew around the edges) or a couple of jumbo snap fasteners or ribbon ties. You could even hand sew a zip into your bag.

To make a belt or tie for your bag, cut a long strip of printed fabric or use a retro school tie or an old belt.

10 Add small lengths of velcro around top edge.

OTHER WAYS TO PIMP YOUR DENIM

Hand painting – go to page 79
Dip dye (suitable only for light-coloured denim) – go to page 67

TWIRLY 'ART' SKIRT

WITH SIDE ZIP

If you want to wear your own 'art', this is the skirt to make. Take an old bed sheet and paint it with textile paints, doodle on it with fabric markers or add embroidery and appliqué patterns or pictures to it. Get creative and design your own fantastic wearable work of art. Then post it to Instagram for everyone to admire!

Alternatively, you could use a seriously fabulous vintage or retro curtain from a carboot sale, charity shop or online auction site. Look out for fabrics from the 1960s in geometric or bold prints. Or choose one from the 1970s in a crazy paisley, exotic floral or even psychedelic pattern. How about using an embroidered tablecloth for a beautiful summer version? You could cut the legs off some old jeans and patch the pieces together (see the instructions for the Denim Dungaree dress on pages 134–49) and then use a brightly coloured zip as a cool detail. You could add a patch pocket (go to pages 94–5), or an appliqué logo (go to pages 43–4) or some embroidery (go to pages 150–51).

Don't worry if you've never sewn a zip into a garment before. I'm going to teach you an easy 'cheat's' method that we use at The Fashion Factory.

WOVEN FABRIC

- ○ Dressmaker's pattern paper
- ○ 1–1.5 metre woven fabric, 150cm wide
- ○ lightweight iron-on interfacing to stiffen the waistband
- ○ 18–20cm closed-end zip with metal teeth in a bright colour (a closed-end zip doesn't open at the end)
- ○ Sewing thread to match fabric
- ○ Sewing thread to match zip tape
- ○ Universal needle, for your sewing machine
- ○ Essential sewing equipment (see pages 12–13)

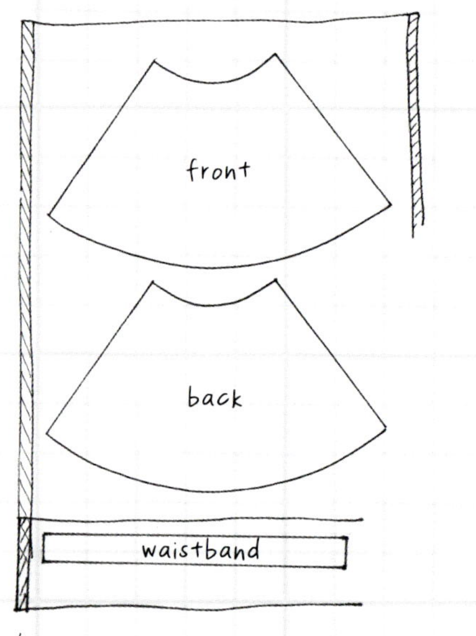

First you need to create your pattern piece so that it's custom made to fit you. It's really easy to do and once you've made the pattern, you can use it again and again. Go to pages 16–21 to learn how to do this.

CUTTING OUT (WOVEN fabrics)

If you've bought new fabric, you'll see it has two cut edges but the sides look different. The finished edges that run up and down the length of the fabric are called SELVEDGES. This is where the fabric was fixed onto the machine that made it. It's important to know where your selvedge is before you start cutting out a garment. The threads or fibres that run from SELVEDGE to SELVEDGE (or right to left across the fabric) are called the WEFT threads. The threads or fibres that run up and down are called the WARP threads. The CENTRE line of your pattern piece must be placed EXACTLY on either the WARP or WEFT of your fabric so that your garment will hang correctly. This is called placing the pattern piece ON GRAIN. It is on the grain of your fabric when lined up with the warp or weft threads.

If you're recycling and can't see a selvedge, then place your CENTRE line exactly in line with the warp or weft threads so that it is ON THE GRAIN OF THE FABRIC. If you look closely at your fabric, you should be able to see the warp and weft threads.

PIN and CUT OUT two SKIRT PANELS. Then CUT OUT your WAISTBAND. This must also be placed ACROSS the fabric and ON GRAIN. CUT OUT the INTERFACING to the same size as your WAISTBAND.

SETTING UP YOUR SEWING MACHINE

FIT a new UNIVERSAL NEEDLE in your sewing machine.

Use a 1.5CM SEAM ALLOWANCE throughout for this skirt. As a guide, PLACE a STRIP of TAPE along the 1.5cm line on the BASE PLATE and use this to LINE UP the RAW EDGE of the FABRIC.

Always BACKSTITCH at the BEGINNING and END of every line of STITCHES.

1 Add any embroidery, logos or patterns to skirt panels.

2 Pin front and back skirt panels with right sides together.

3 Sew side seam from waist to hem with 1.5cm seam allowance.

Zigzag stitch raw seam edges and press open.

MAKING THE SKIRT

1 If you want to ADD any EMBROIDERY, LOGOS or PATTERNS to your skirt panels, do this now. GO TO PAGES 42–3 and 150–51 to learn how to do this.

2 PLACE the SKIRT PANELS with RIGHT SIDES TOGETHER. PIN along one SIDE SEAM, noting the direction of the pins.

3 Using a regular STRAIGHT STITCH and a 1.5CM SEAM ALLOWANCE (with the EDGE of the FABRIC to the EDGE of the TAPE on the base plate) SEW the SIDE SEAM from the WAIST down to the HEM. BACKSTITCH at each end.

4 Set your sewing machine to a medium-large ZIGZAG STITCH and sew the RAW EDGES of your SEAM ALLOWANCE to stop them fraying.

STEAM PRESS the seam OPEN and flat.

ADDING STAY STITCHING

Set your sewing machine to a regular STRAIGHT STITCH, but make the stitch length slightly LONGER. SEW a line of STRAIGHT STITCHES 1cm in from the waist edge on both skirt panels. BACKSTITCH at each end. This is called STAY STITCHING and stops the waistline stretching.

STEAM PRESS the panels flat.

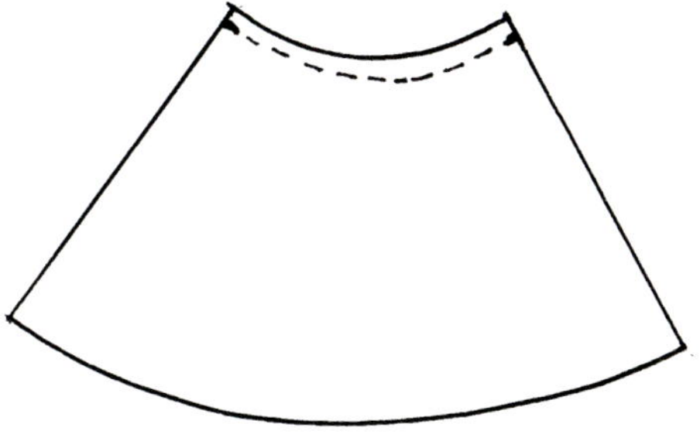

5 Apply interfacing to waistband, fold in half and press.

6 Gently gather skirt panels to fit waistband.

7 Pin waistband to skirt panels.

TIP

Once you've added your waistband then try the skirt on. Pin the side seam together. You need to keep a 1.5cm seam allowance but any excess can be trimmed down now.

MAKING THE WAISTBAND

PLACE the iron-on INTERFACING with the SHINY SIDE (glue side) facing up. PLACE the WAISTBAND on top of the interfacing RIGHT SIDE UP. You are fixing the INTERFACING to the REVERSE of the WAISTBAND.

Set your iron to a MEDIUM heat. HOLD the iron on the waistband fabric for a FEW SECONDS or until the glue has MELTED and the interfacing has fused to the fabric.

5 FOLD your waistband in half LENGTHWAYS and PRESS to form a sharp CREASE.

ATTACHING THE WAISTBAND

6 Place your skirt RIGHT SIDE UP. LAY the WAISTBAND on top RIGHT SIDE DOWN against the WAIST EDGE of the skirt. PLACE the two RAW EDGES TOGETHER.

7 Starting at the left side, PIN all the way along. Make sure that the two edges are perfectly together.

Set your sewing machine to a regular STRAIGHT STITCH. SEW all the way along. Keep checking that NO PLEATS are forming UNDERNEATH your sewing. BACKSTITCH at each end.

8 Press waist seam upwards.

9 Fold waistband over along crease. Pin and stitch through layers.

10 Pin and stitch side seam from waist to hem.

11 Zigzag stitch raw seam edges. Press seam open.

8 STEAM PRESS the seam allowance upwards.

Using a medium ZIGZAG STITCH, sew along the other RAW EDGE of the WAISTBAND to stop it fraying. STEAM PRESS flat.

9 With the skirt RIGHT SIDE UP, FOLD the WAISTBAND over along the CREASE. Keeping it flat, PIN through ALL THE LAYERS just ABOVE the WAIST SEAM.

SEW all the way along on the EDGE of the WAISTBAND. Sew slowly and keep your stitching neat.

STEAM PRESS flat. If the waistband has stretched, TRIM away the end.

STITCHING THE SIDE SEAM

10 FOLD your skirt panels in HALF with RIGHT SIDES TOGETHER. PIN the SIDE SEAM from the WAIST to the HEM.

SEW the SIDE SEAM from the WAIST to the HEM. BACKSTITCH at each end.

11 Set your sewing machine to a medium-large ZIGZAG STITCH and sew the two RAW EDGES of your seam allowance to stop them from fraying.

STEAM PRESS the seam OPEN and flat.

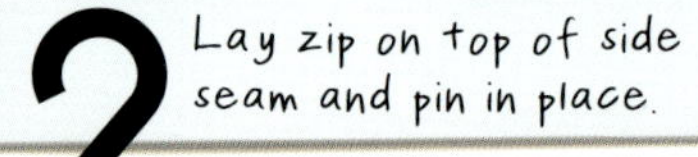

12 Lay zip on top of side seam and pin in place.

13

Zigzag stitch zip tape with presser foot against metal teeth.

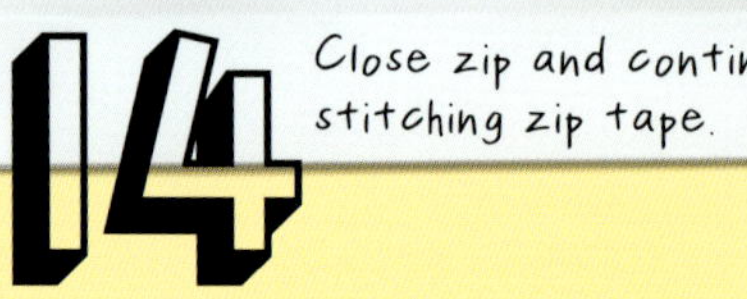

14 Close zip and continue stitching zip tape.

HOW TO:
ADD A ZIP

ADDING THE SIDE ZIP

(12) Turn the skirt so it is right side out. LAY your ZIP on top of the SIDE SEAM. FOLD OVER the TOP of the ZIP TAPE inside the skirt and PIN all the way down one side to the END of the ZIP. Make sure the teeth of the zip sit exactly on the SEAM LINE all the way down.

OPEN the zip HALF WAY.

Thread your sewing machine with a colour to match your zip tape.

(13) Set your sewing machine to a large ZIGZAG STITCH.

PLACE the LEFT SIDE of the PRESSER FOOT against the side of the metal ZIP TEETH. BACKSTITCH. SEW from the TOP down to the ZIP PULL. STOP just BEFORE the ZIP PULL.

(14) TURN the HANDWHEEL of your machine towards you until the POINT of the NEEDLE is through the FABRIC. LIFT the PRESSER FOOT and CLOSE the ZIP.

LOWER the PRESSER FOOT and continue sewing to the END of the ZIP. Keep the PRESSER FOOT against the side of the metal ZIP TEETH at all time. BACKSTITCH at the end.

REPEAT on the OTHER SIDE of the ZIP.

DESIGN
IDEA

For a cute 'matching set', make a top in the same fabric using the paper pattern that comes with this book. You could add a matching or denim bib and braces like the Denim Dungaree Dress on pages 134–49. How about a fabulous metallic version for parties?

15 Stitch along bottom of zip tape twice.

16 Open zip and cut open side seam behind zip.

17 Trim away any excess fabric from zip tape.

18 Turn under 1cm all round hem edge.

15 SEW a row of small ZIGZAG STITCHES across the BOTTOM END of the ZIP TAPE twice. BACKSTITCH. TRIM all the loose threads.

16 OPEN the zip ALL THE WAY. Using a seam ripper or scissors, CUT the SIDE SEAM open behind the zip.

STEAM PRESS the zip on the reverse side.

FINISHING THE HEM

18 TURN UNDER 1cm all round the HEM EDGE. PIN. Use a measuring tape to keep your hem even.

Set your sewing machine to a large ZIGZAG STITCH. Using a sewing thread to match your fabric and starting at a side seam, PLACE the right side of the PRESSER FOOT on the EDGE of the FOLD and SEW all the way round the HEM. BACKSTITCH at each end. As the hem line is curved, it may help you sew more neatly if you GENTLY PULL the fabric both to the front and back of the presser foot as you go.

If your hem line stretches during sewing, HOVER a STEAM IRON just above the fabric and STEAM WELL until the fabric gently SHRINKS back into place.

PATCH POCKET

The patch pocket is a great way of adding a cool detail to your dress, top or skirt. They look great in a contrast fabric and can be made in various shapes. On the pattern sheet that comes with this book, you'll find a patch pocket template to trace off and use.

You can use pretty much any kind of woven fabric to make these pockets (stretch fabrics can be used, but I wouldn't recommend that to a beginner). You will also need a little bit of lightweight iron-on interfacing. An old embroidered napkin makes a really cute patch pocket.

MAKING THE PATCH POCKET

1 PIN and CUT out round your pocket pattern piece. Make sure it's ON GRAIN (see page 22). CUT out a 3.5cm-deep strip of IRON-ON INTERFACING the same width as your pocket. With your pocket RIGHT SIDE DOWN, place the interfacing SHINY SIDE DOWN (glue side) on the TOP EDGE of your pocket. With a medium-hot IRON, press until the GLUE is MELTED and it's completely FIXED.

2 FOLD BACK the TOP EDGE by 3.5cm. PRESS and PIN.

3 With a 1cm seam allowance, STITCH both sides of the folded-back section. BACKSTITCH at each end.

4 TURN RIGHT SIDE OUT and push the corners out to form two neat corners. Press flat, then turn the other four edges under by 1cm and press.

5 If you want to, you can add a row of stitching across the pocket through both layers. This could be straight, zigzag or an embroidery stitch.

ATTACHING THE PATCH POCKET

1 Pin your pocket in place. Try on your garment. Check your pocket is in the right place and at the correct angle.

2 With a sharp needle in your machine you can now edge stitch round your pocket. Backstitch well at each end. Pivot at the corners (see page 33). Try to keep the same distance from the edge all the way round.

DESIGN IDEA

Use a large zigzag stitch or a machine embroidery stitch as a detail. How about doing two rows of straight stitch to get a 'twin needle' look as on jeans?

CAP SLEEVE PICTURE TOP

This is a fairly easy top to make and a chance to get 'arty' and design a unique front panel. Think of the front panel as your blank canvas. Because we use a woven fabric (rather than a stretchy one) for the front, you can add a pattern, print, picture or logo to your own design (go to pages 43–4). Alternatively, get creative with machine embroidery (go to pages 150–51). Or how about making a modern patchwork front panel (go to pages 104–5)?

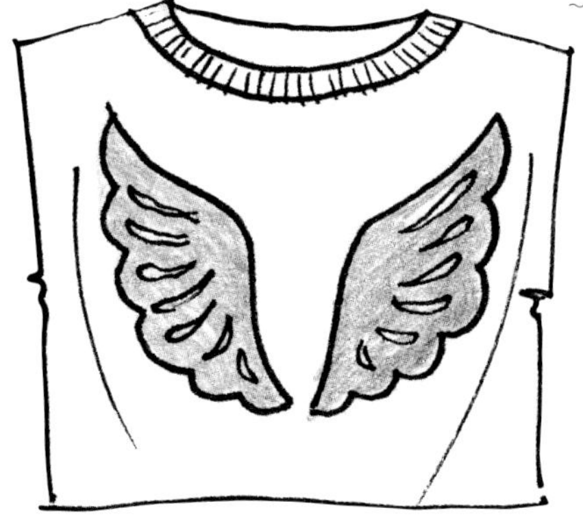

We are using a stretch fabric for the back panel. You could make a shorter 'cropped' version or a longer 'tunic' version by lengthening or shortening your pattern piece.

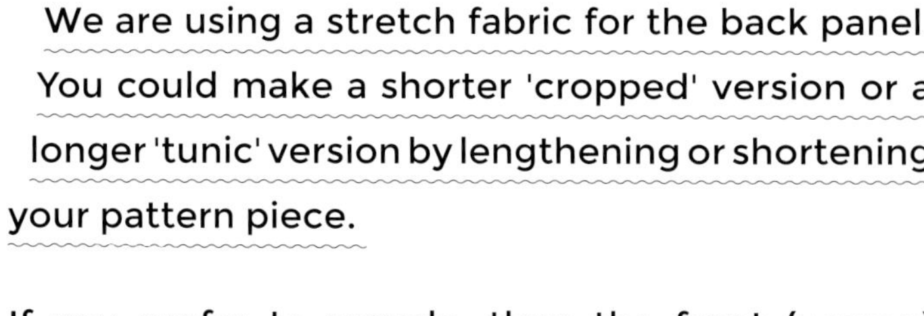

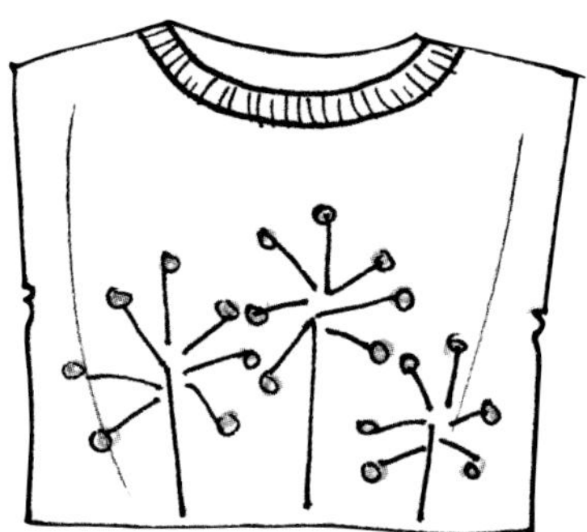

If you prefer to recycle, then the front (woven) and back (stretch) panels could be made from second-hand fabric or upcycled clothing. I've used a black polyester cotton sheet I bought from a carboot sale. Why not make yourself a 'set' with a matching skater skirt afterwards?

WOVEN FRONT/
STRETCH BACK

- ○ Dressmaker's pattern paper
- ○ Light- or mediumweight woven fabric, for front panel
- ○ Light- or mediumweight stretch fabric, for back panel and neckband
- ○ Lightweight iron-on interfacing (to go behind your picture)
- ○ Universal needle, for your sewing machine
- ○ Freestyle embroidery machine foot
- ○ Contrasting and matching sewing thread
- ○ Essential sewing equipment (see pages 12-13)

★★★★★★★★★★★★★★★★★★★★★

SETTING UP YOUR SEWING MACHINE

FIT a sharp, new UNIVERSAL NEEDLE in your machine.

Use a 1CM SEAM ALLOWANCE throughout for this top. As a guide, PLACE the RIGHT EDGE of the PRESSER FOOT on the RAW EDGE of the FABRIC or PLACE a STRIP of TAPE along the 1cm line on the BASE PLATE and use this to LINE UP the RAW EDGE of the FABRIC.

Always BACKSTITCH at the BEGINNING and END of every line of STITCHES.

Read the sections on pinning and cutting on pages 22-3. This will help you to cut out your fabric pieces without making any mistakes.

For this project you need to use PATTERN A, which you'll find on the pattern sheet that comes with this book. Make sure you take your chest measurement first and use the correct size (see pages 14-5). TRACE off your size onto dressmaker's pattern paper. You need the FRONT, the BACK and the NECKBAND.

CUTTING OUT YOUR TOP

LAY out your woven and stretch fabrics on a flat surface. FOLD the fabrics in half. Place the CENTRE line of your FRONT and BACK pattern pieces (where it says 'place on fold of fabric') exactly on the fabric FOLDS. PIN. Make sure the FRONT pattern piece is ON GRAIN (see page 22). Make sure the NECKBAND pattern piece is ACROSS the stretch of the fabric so that it stretches in length but not width.

CUT out one FRONT panel from WOVEN fabric, then one BACK panel and one NECKBAND from STRETCH fabric. Place your neckband pattern ACROSS the STRETCH of the fabric, so that it will only stretch in length NOT in width.

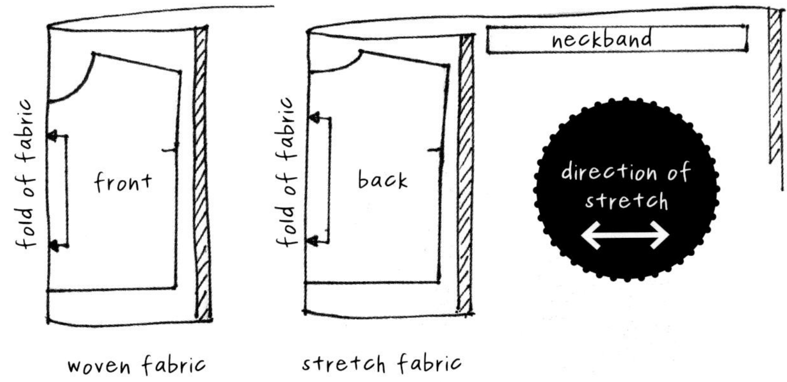

Using tailor's chalk, MARK the NOTCHES at the bottom of the ARMHOLES on both the FRONT and BACK. MARK the MID-POINT NECKLINE on the FRONT for matching up the neckband.

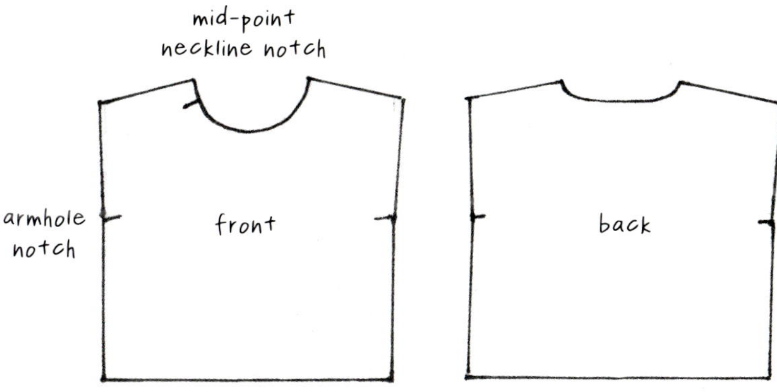

ADDING YOUR DESIGN

You can add a design in many different ways. Appliqué, machine embroidery or freestyle embroidery. To add a design like the one shown here, follow these steps:

1 DRAW your DESIGN on paper. LAY your DRAWING ON TOP of your FRONT panel to get an idea of scale. Do NOT go too close to the edges or your design may disappear when the seams are sewn.

TAPE your DRAWING to a WINDOW, then tape the FRONT panel ON TOP. Using tailor's chalk, TRACE the DESIGN onto your fabric.

CUT OUT a piece of lightweight iron-on INTERFACING big enough to cover your entire design. PLACE it SHINY SIDE DOWN (glue side) on the REVERSE of your FRONT panel. Set your iron to a medium heat. HOLD the IRON on the interfacing for a few seconds or until the glue has melted and the interfacing has fused to the fabric.

EMBROIDER your design. GO TO PAGES 102–3 to learn how to do FREESTYLE EMBROIDERY. Next, PRESS well and continue to follow the instructions below.

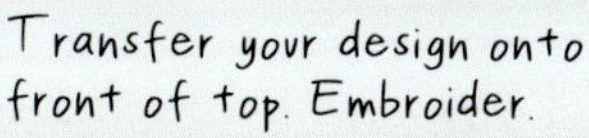
1 Transfer your design onto front of top. Embroider.

MAKING YOUR TOP

2 Replace your REGULAR machine foot. Place your FRONT and BACK panels RIGHT SIDES TOGETHER (woven fabric on top) and PIN one SHOULDER as shown. With a 1cm seam allowance, STRAIGHT STITCH the shoulder seam from NECK to SHOULDER. BACKSTITCH at each end. ZIGZAG STITCH along the seam allowance to finish the raw edges.

PRESS the seam allowance towards the BACK of your top.

2 Stitch one shoulder seam.

3 Attach the neckband.

4 Pin together side seams from armhole notches to hem.

Sew side seam. Do not stitch above armhole notch.

DESIGN
IDEA

You could make a dress version of this top by making it a bit longer to wear with leggings or with jeans and boots. A lightweight, lacey or bright version could be worn with bare legs and sandals in the Summer. You could make a set – a waist-length or cropped version with matching skater skirt (see page 50).

ATTACHING THE NECKBAND

3 Now GO TO 'Adding the Neckband' on page 118, then continue to follow the instructions below.

PIN the second shoulder seam, with the stretch fabric on top. With a 1cm seam allowance, STRAIGHT STITCH the shoulder seam from NECK TO SHOULDER. BACKSTITCH at each end. ZIGZAG STITCH along the seam allowance to finish the raw edges.

PRESS the seam allowance towards the BACK of your top.

SEWING THE SIDE SEAMS

Using a large ZIGZAG STITCH, stitch along the THREE EDGES of your FRONT WOVEN panel to stop any fraying. PRESS flat.

4 With RIGHT SIDES TOGETHER, PIN the sides BELOW the ARMHOLE notches (marked on paper pattern).

5 With a 1cm seam allowance, STRAIGHT STITCH the SIDE SEAMS from the ARMHOLE NOTCH down to the HEM. BACKSTITCH at each end. Do NOT sew ABOVE the ARMHOLE NOTCH.

PRESS the seam open and flat.

REPEAT for the other side seam.

6 Remove accessory tray to reveal free arm.

7

Zigzag stitch all round armholes right on edge of folds.

Zigzag stitching on edge of folds to create tiny scallops.

FINISHING THE ARMHOLES

TURN UNDER 1cm all round the ARMHOLE EDGES and PIN.

6 REMOVE the accessory tray from your sewing machine to reveal the free arm.

7 SLIDE the ARMHOLE onto the FREE ARM. Set your sewing machine to a large ZIGZAG STITCH.

8 Starting at the BOTTOM of the ARMHOLE, at the SIDE SEAM, STITCH all the way round the ARMHOLE EDGE right ON the EDGE of the FOLD to create a tiny scalloped edge.

9 Turn under 1cm around hem and zigzag stitch.

FINISHING THE HEM

9 TURN UNDER at least 1cm all round the HEM EDGE to achieve the top length you require. PIN as shown.

Set your sewing machine to a large ZIGZAG STITCH. Using a sewing thread to match your fabric, starting and finishing at a side seam, SEW right ON the EDGE of the FOLD to make a tiny scalloped edge.

STEAM PRESS the hem and armhole edges.

If your hem line stretches during sewing, HOVER a STEAM IRON just above the fabric and STEAM WELL until the fabric gently SHRINKS back into place.

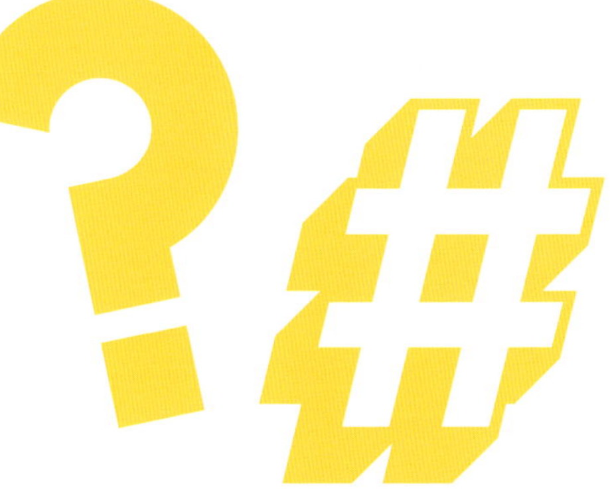

FREESTYLE
EMBROIDERY
MAD AND MESSY!

With freestyle embroidery, you can create pretty much any design you want on fabric. This style of embroidery has a loose, messy look to it and gives a creative feel to a project. You'll need a freestyle embroidery foot for your sewing machine, which you can easily buy online or at your local haberdashers. Remove the standard foot from your machine – they usually unscrew at one side – and then attach your freestyle foot.

You can place your fabric in an embroidery hoop for stitching, if it's a fairly big piece, but it's quite easy to freestyle embroider fabric without a hoop.

1 Using a pencil or tailor's chalk, draw your design onto your fabric.

2 Iron interfacing (glue side down) onto the back of the fabric.

3 Attach a freestyle embroidery foot. Set your machine to a straight stitch and the stitch length dial to '0'.

4 Work a few stitches on the spot instead of backstitching. Trim any long thread ends. Move your fabric slowly and trace over your design with the needle. If you want the design to be very bold, go over it a few times.
Steam press.

TIP

Don't look away when you're working freestyle embroidery. Keep your fingers well away from the needle. Practise on a scrap of fabric first.

MODERN PATCHWORK

Patchwork was extremely popular in the 1970s and is now making a comeback. It's also a great way of using up scraps of fabric. You can create some fabulous combinations with patchwork. To make it really special, once your patchwork is complete, you could add freestyle embroidery on top. We make lots of patchwork bags at The Fashion Factory and they always look amazing.

The easiest kind of patchwork to make is a grid of squares. To do this, cut out lots of squares all the same size from fabrics of similar weights. All the edges must be of equal length.

1

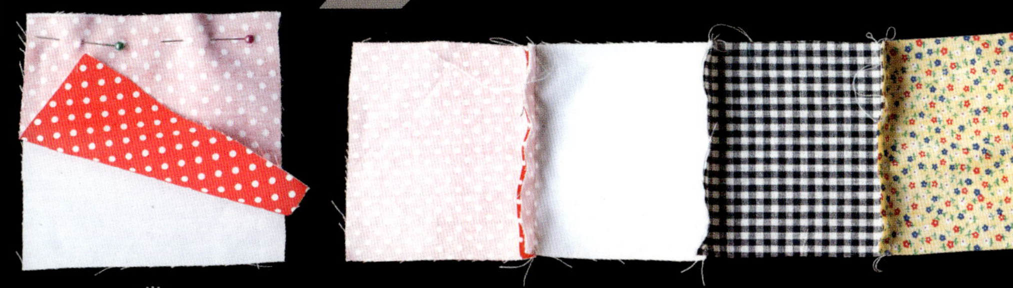

1 Carefully cut out as many same-size fabric squares as you need. Arrange the squares in the order you want them in your patchwork. Avoid putting the same fabrics together in rows.

Start with the top row. Pin the side edges of all the adjacent squares with right sides together.

With the edge of the presser foot to the edge of the fabric, straight stitch each seam. Backstitch at both ends.

Repeat for every row.

Flip all the rows over so that they are now right side down.

2 Press the seam allowances of the top row to the left. Press the seam allowances of the second row to the right, the third row to the left, the fourth row to the right. Repeat for every row.

3 Now pin the top row to the second row with right sides together and stitch each seam. Place the pins so that your machine doesn't push your seam allowances the wrong way when you stitch over them.

Repeat for every row until your patchwork panel is complete. Press the seam allowances flat.

Either leave your patchwork plain or add some embroidery on top.

3

FLARED SKATER DRESS

LEVEL 2 PROJECT

Very easy and quick to make, this is a great casual dress for all year round. Choose a really fabulous print in a light- to mediumweight woven fabric and make it über cool with contrasting or matching edgings. A viscose or polyester works well, but you could also use a cotton or a poly-cotton blend.

How about using a different print for the top and skirt panels and really mixing it up? A baby cord version with patch pockets for the winter looks cute while a shiny, metallic fabric is amazing for special occasions.

I've used a printed black-and-white fabric, which I've customised with textile paint. You could use an old cotton sheet and paint on your own designs or tie dye (go to page 68).

You can wear this style loose or add ties to the sides to create a more fitted shape at the waist.

- Dressmaker's pattern paper
- 1.75–2m fabric, 150cm wide (if you're tall, you'll need slightly more fabric)
- Sewing thread to match fabric
- 1.5m bias binding, 12mm wide, for neck and armhole edges
- Sewing thread to match bias binding
- Ribbon ties (optional)
- Universal needle for sewing machine
- Essential sewing equipment (see pages 12–13)

★★★★★★★★★★★★★★★★★★★★★★

SETTING UP YOUR SEWING MACHINE

FIT a new, sharp UNIVERSAL NEEDLE in your sewing machine.

Use a 1CM SEAM ALLOWANCE throughout for this dress. As a guide, PLACE the RIGHT EDGE of the PRESSER FOOT on the RAW EDGE of the FABRIC or PLACE a STRIP of TAPE along the 1cm line on the BASE PLATE and use this to LINE UP the RAW EDGE of the FABRIC.

Always BACKSTITCH at the BEGINNING and END of every line of STITCHES.

For this project you need to use PATTERN B, which you'll find on the pattern sheet that comes with this book. Make sure you take your chest measurement first and use the correct size (see pages 14–5). TRACE off your size onto dressmaker's pattern paper. You need the FRONT BODICE and the BACK BODICE. You'll also need to use a SKIRT PATTERN that you make yourself. Go to 21 to learn how to do this.

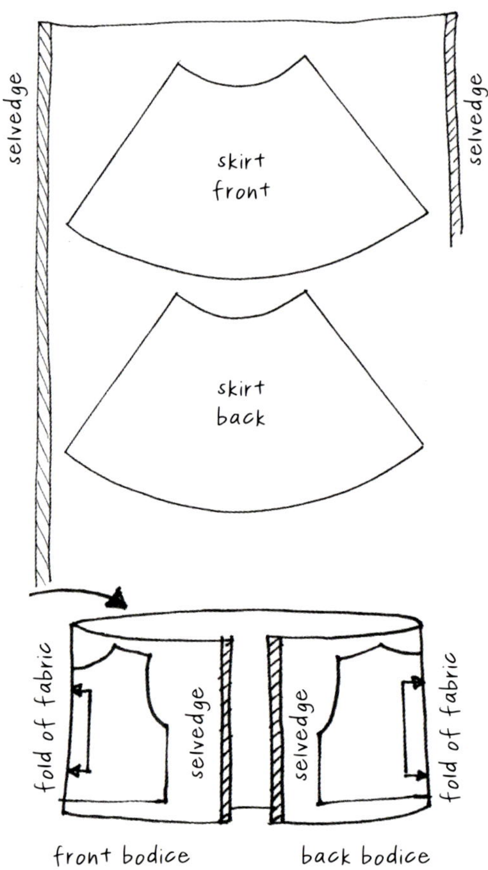

CUTTING OUT YOUR DRESS

LAY your FABRIC out FLAT. PLACE the SKIRT pattern pieces ON GRAIN on the fabric. PIN and carefully CUT OUT the two SKIRT PANELS. If you're unsure about how to do this, go to pages 22–3 and read the sections on PINNING and CUTTING OUT.

Take the remaining fabric and FOLD the sides in to the middle. PLACE the CENTRE line of your FRONT BODICE and BACK BODICE pattern pieces (where it says 'place on fold of fabric') exactly on the fabric FOLDS and ON GRAIN. The CENTRE lines must be PARALLEL to the SELVEDGES.

ADDING BUST DARTS (for all sizes, except size 1)

If you need to create bust darts do this now. Go to page 34 to learn how to do this. If you don't need bust darts, go straight to step 1.

ADDING STAY STITCHING

Set your sewing machine to a regular STRAIGHT STITCH. SEW a line of STRAIGHT STITCHES 1cm in from the WAIST EDGE on BOTH skirt panels. BACKSTITCH at each end. This is called STAY STITCHING and stops the panels from stretching.

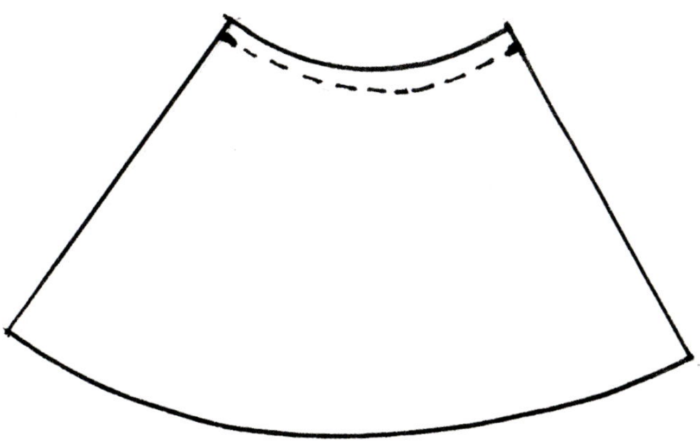

DESIGN **IDEA**

Once you've cut out your bodice and skirt panels, you can add your own customised design. You could tie dye or hand paint your fabric using textile paints or add a lace panel. Go to page 75 to learn how to do this.

1 Pin and stitch skirt and bodice panels together along waist.

2

Trim away any excess fabric from skirt panels if they stretch.

Zigzag stitch raw edges to stop them fraying.

3

ATTACHING THE BODICE TO THE SKIRT

PLACE the FRONT BODICE and BACK BODICE panels RIGHT SIDES UP and with NECK EDGES facing towards you.

(1) Place a SKIRT panel ON TOP of each bodice panel RIGHT SIDES DOWN, matching the WAIST EDGES. PIN together at RIGHT ANGLES to the EDGES. Space the pins 2cm apart, with their points just over the edge of the fabric. WORK from one EDGE to the OTHER. Make sure that the two RAW EDGES are TOGETHER all the way along.

With a 1cm seam allowance, STITCH over the pins until the bodice and skirt are attached. BACKSTITCH at both ends.

(2) Once joined, if the SKIRT PANELS have STRETCHED and are wider than the bodice, TRIM away the excess. Trim the SAME AMOUNT from each edge down to the hem.

(3) Set your sewing machine to a medium-large ZIGZAG STITCH and sew the RAW EDGES of your seam allowances together to stop them from fraying. PRESS the waist seam allowances UPWARDS towards the bodice of the dress.

Pin and stitch shoulder seams. Zigzag stitch raw edges.

4

Pin and stitch side seams from armholes to hem.

5

Zigzag stitch raw edges and press seams towards back.

6

SEWING THE SHOULDER SEAMS

4 PLACE the FRONT BODICE and BACK BODICE panels RIGHT SIDES TOGETHER. PIN along both SHOULDER SEAMS.

Set your sewing machine to a STRAIGHT STITCH. With a 1cm seam allowance, SEW from the NECK edges to the ARMHOLE edges. BACKSTITCH at each end.

Set your sewing machine to a medium-large ZIGZAG STITCH and sew the RAW EDGES of your seam allowances together. PRESS the shoulder seams towards the BACK of the garment.

SEWING THE SIDE SEAMS

5 LINE UP the WAIST SEAMS on the Front and Back bodice panels. PIN along the SIDE SEAMS from the ARMHOLES to the HEM.

Set your sewing machine to a STRAIGHT STITCH. With a 1cm seam allowance, SEW from the ARMHOLE edges to the HEM. BACKSTITCH at each end.

6 Set your sewing machine to a medium-large ZIGZAG STITCH and sew the RAW EDGES of your seam allowances together to stop them from fraying. PRESS the side seams towards the BACK of the garment.

DESIGN IDEA

You could even use a machine embroidery stitch on top of your binding instead of a zigzag.

Open out and pin bias binding round neckline and armholes. 7

Fold bias binding over to inside of dress and pin. 8

HOW TO: ADD BIAS BINDING

9

Zigzag stitch bias binding in place all round neck and armholes.

10 Turn under 1cm all round hem edge.

FINISHING THE NECKLINE AND ARMHOLES

7 Turn your dress RIGHT SIDE OUT. Starting and finishing at the CENTRE BACK of the NECKLINE, OPEN OUT the BIAS BINDING and pin all round the opening with RIGHT SIDES TOGETHER. The pins should be no more than 2cm apart and the edges flat together.

SEW the bias binding IN THE CREASE nearest to the raw neck edge using a STRAIGHT STITCH. SEW SLOWLY over the pins. When you arrive back at the start, OVERLAP the bias binding by approximately 1cm. Remove the pins.

8 FOLD the BIAS BINDING in half over the neckline edge towards the inside of the dress. PIN in place.

9 SEW the edge of the BIAS BINDING all the way round the neckline. At The Fashion Factory we use a large ZIGZAG STITCH because it's easier than straight stitch. BACKSTITCH at each end.

Repeat steps 7–9 for the armholes. Start and finish at the underarm side seam.

FINISHING THE HEM

10 TURN UNDER 1cm all round the HEM EDGE. PIN. Use a measuring tape to keep your hem even.

Bias binding comes in a variety of different widths and colours. It's very useful for finishing edges that are curved, because it bends well.

Zigzag stitch all round the hem edge.

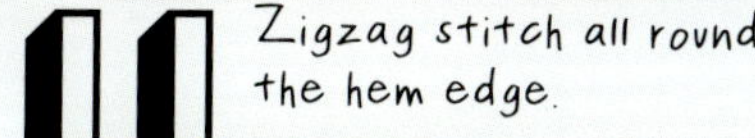

12

Pin side ties at waist seam, facing front, leaving 1cm at back.

Fold side ties over towards back and stitch ends.

13

11 Set your sewing machine to a large ZIGZAG STITCH. Using a sewing thread to match your fabric, starting and finishing at a side seam, SEW along the RAW HEM EDGE. STRETCH the fabric slightly both in FRONT and BEHIND the PRESSER FOOT to stop the hem from unfolding. This helps to keep the hem curved. BACKSTITCH at each end.

If your hem line stretches during sewing, HOVER a STEAM IRON just above the fabric and STEAM and PRESS WELL until the fabric SHRINKS gently back into place. TRIM away any LOOSE THREADS.

TIP

If you get a 'bubble' of fabric in the hem as you sew, slide a pin along the fabric horizontally towards and then under the needle to create a tiny pleat and flatten the excess fabric.

ADDING THE SIDE TIES (optional)

To give your dress a more fitted shape, add some ribbon at the side seams to tie at the back.

12 PIN the SIDE TIES at the WAIST SEAM, facing the front, with 1cm towards the back. Set your sewing machine to a STRAIGHT STITCH. SEW across the SIDE TIES just a few millimetres from the end.

13 FOLD the SIDE TIES back on themselves and SEW a SECOND line of STITCHES 0.5–1cm from the end.

CAP SLEEVE TUNIC

LEVEL 2 PROJECT

This is a nice simple tunic top that can be worn on its own or over leggings. A mediumweight knitted stretch fabric or sweatshirt fabric works very well for this style. There are a couple of types of sweatshirt fabric to look out for: a fleece-back version with a soft brushed back and a loop-back version. I prefer the loop-back version. For this project, use a simple hand-printing method on the sweatshirt fabric. You can learn how to do this on page 124.

Another option is to use a woven fabric for the tunic front and a stretch fabric for the back. A modern patchwork or a printed fabric would look great. Whichever way you choose to make this tunic, keep a balance in your fabric weights at the front and back.

To make this shape, use the Pattern A that you'll find on the pattern sheet that comes with this book. Although the pattern is for a top, I'll show you how to create the tunic shape by drawing directly onto your fabric with tailor's chalk.

54

- ○ Dressmaker's pattern paper
- ○ Mediumweight sweatshirt fabric (the length required, plus 10cm)
- ○ Rib fabric, for neckband
- ○ Woven fabric, such as poly-cotton, for the side pockets (optional)
- ○ Stretch or ballpoint needle, for your sewing machine
- ○ Sewing thread to match fabric
- ○ Essential sewing equipment (see pages 12–13)

★★★★★★★★★★★★★★★★★★★★

SETTING UP YOUR SEWING MACHINE

FIT a new STRETCH or BALLPOINT NEEDLE in your sewing machine.

Use a 1CM SEAM ALLOWANCE throughout for this tunic. As a guide, PLACE the RIGHT EDGE of the PRESSER FOOT on the RAW EDGE of the FABRIC or PLACE a STRIP of TAPE along the 1cm line on the BASE PLATE and use this to LINE UP the RAW EDGE of the FABRIC.

Always BACKSTITCH at the BEGINNING and END of every line of STITCHES.

For this project you need to use PATTERN A, which you'll find on the pattern sheet that comes with this book. Make sure you take your chest measurement first and use the correct size (see pages 14–5). TRACE off your size onto dressmaker's pattern paper. You need the FRONT, the BACK and the NECKBAND. If you are adding SIDE POCKETS, then you need that piece too.

CUTTING OUT YOUR TUNIC

Decide on the LENGTH you want your TUNIC. Using a measuring tape, MEASURE down from your NECK POINT (where your neck meets your shoulder). ADD 4cm to this measurement. Call this MEASUREMENT A.

LAY out your fabric on a flat surface. FOLD the SIDES in to the middle, as shown. Place the CENTRE line of your FRONT and BACK pattern pieces (where it says 'place on fold of fabric') exactly on the fabric FOLDS. PIN.

Measuring from the NECK POINT of the pattern pieces, MARK the fabric in tailor's chalk at the length of MEASUREMENT A.

Using a ruler, EXTEND the SIDE SEAMS and DRAW the HEMLINES at RIGHT ANGLES. CUT OUT your FRONT and BACK panels.

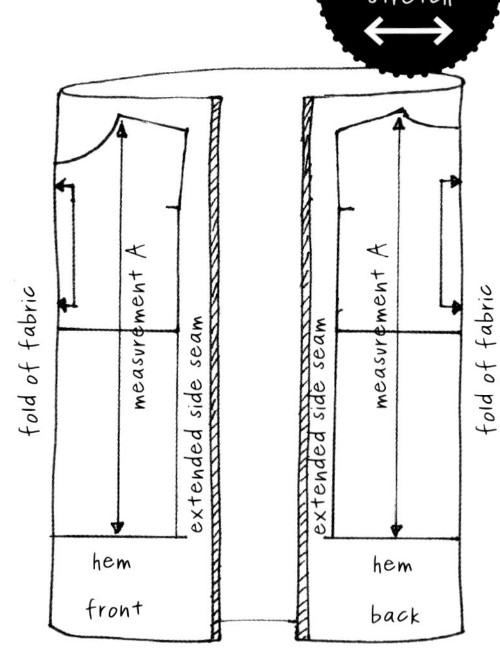

This pattern uses a ribbed neckband (like you see on T-shirts), so you need to buy a small amount of RIB FABRIC. If you can't find rib fabric in the colour you want, use a stretchy jersey fabric.

PIN the NECKBAND pattern piece onto the rib fabric, noting the direction of stretch. CUT OUT the NECKBAND.

MARK an ARMHOLE NOTCH on BOTH SIDES of the FRONT and BACK panels with tailor's chalk.

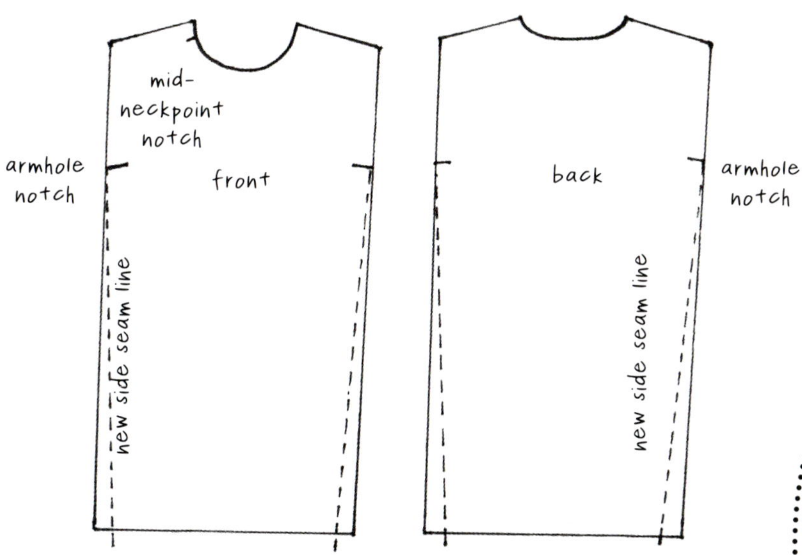

Now the Front and Back are cut out, you can make your tunic a SLIMMER SHAPE by DECREASING the width of the HEM. Using tailor's chalk and a ruler, DRAW new SIDE SEAMS on the Front and Back panels. Start just BELOW the ARMHOLE NOTCH and ANGLE the lines slightly INWARDS. Make sure all side seams are the same. TRIM carefully along the lines.

If you want to ADD any PRINTING, APPLIQUÉ or EMBROIDERY to your FRONT panel, or if you want to add SIDE POCKETS, do it NOW. Go to pages 46, 102 and 124 to learn how to do this. When finished, STEAM PRESS the FRONT panel FLAT.

TIP

Use a STRAIGHT STRETCH STITCH, which allows the seam to stretch. The needle works two stitches forward, then one stitch backwards and repeats. If your machine doesn't have a stretch stitch, set it to a SMALL ZIGZAG STITCH. Work a TEST PIECE first on a scrap of jersey fabric. Does your seam look okay? Are the stitches too big? If so, change your stitch length dial until it looks right.

HOW TO: ADD A NECKBAND

2

Mark mid-point notch on front neckline using tailor's chalk.

3

Fold neckband in half lengthways and mark centre with pin.

4

Match neckband centre to mid-point notch on neckline.

1

Pin and stitch front and back panels at one shoulder.

TIP

The neckband is fixed to the neckline AFTER one shoulder seam has been stitched and BEFORE the second shoulder seam is sewn.

MAKING THE TUNIC

If you're using a WOVEN FABRIC (non-stretch fabric) for the FRONT panel, first set your sewing machine to a medium-large ZIGZAG STITCH and SEW round all the RAW EDGES to stop them from fraying. STEAM PRESS the edges FLAT.

1 Place the FRONT and BACK panels RIGHT SIDES TOGETHER and PIN one SHOULDER SEAM. Set your sewing machine to a STRAIGHT STRETCH STITCH or small ZIGZAG STITCH. With a 1cm seam allowance, SEW from the NECK edge to the ARMHOLE edge. BACKSTITCH at each end.

PRESS the SEAM towards the BACK of the tunic.

2 Using tailor's chalk, MARK the mid-point neckline notch on the FRONT panel just in front of the shoulder seam. It's marked on the paper pattern.

ADDING THE NECKBAND

3 FOLD the NECKBAND in half lengthways to find the CENTRE point. MARK with a PIN.

4 MATCH the CENTRE point of the NECKBAND to the MID-POINT NOTCH on your FRONT NECKLINE. PLACE the RAW EDGES TOGETHER and PIN.

5 Stretch and pin neckband to neckline.

6 Slowly stitch neckband in place, s-t-r-e-t-c-h-i-n-g as you sew.

7 Finish raw edges with zigzag stitch to stop fraying.

Now PIN the ENDS of the NECKBAND to the CORNERS of the NECKLINE.

5 PULL both ends of the NECKBAND to stretch the rib flat. Ask someone else to help. PIN the NECKBAND to the NECKLINE, keeping all raw edges together.

6 Set your sewing machine to a STRAIGHT STRETCH STITCH or a small ZIGZAG STITCH. With the EDGE of the PRESSER FOOT to the EDGE of the FABRIC, start at one end and sew SLOWLY. Make sure you S-T-R-E-T-C-H the rib as you sew. At every pin, STOP and CHECK UNDERNEATH that you're sewing only through the THREE LAYERS. Keep stretching them together. BACKSTITCH at each end.

7 FINISH the RAW EDGES with a large ZIGZAG STITCH to stop them from fraying.

If it hasn't worked out, carefully cut along your stitch line to remove the neckband. Prepare a new neckband and have another go.

8 Once the neckband is attached, PIN the second SHOULDER SEAM and STITCH. BACKSTITCH at each end.

Pin and stitch the second shoulder seam.

8

TIP

If your sewing machine skips a few stitches at the join between the rib and fabric, backstitch so that you don't leave a gap in your shoulder seam.

Mark point of pocket tops on side seams.

10

11

Place pocket bags against side seams with right sides together.

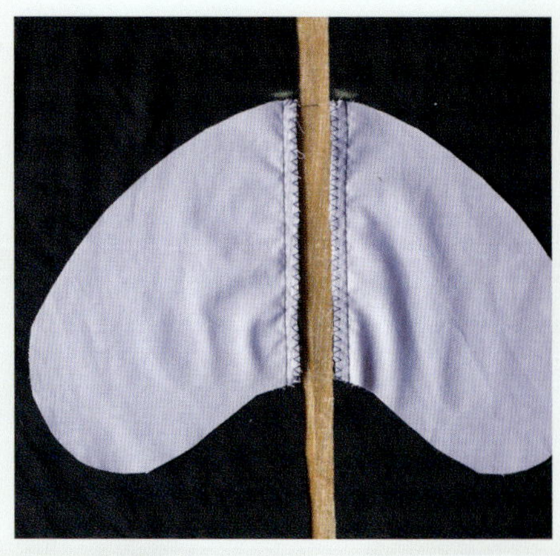

12

Sew pocket bags in place on garment side seams.

Pin and stitch side seams from armhole notch to hem.

9

HOW TO:
ADD A SIDE POCKET

SEWING THE SIDE SEAMS (without pockets)

9 PIN the SIDE SEAMS with RIGHT SIDES TOGETHER. With a 1cm seam allowance, SEW down from the ARMHOLE NOTCH to the HEM. BACKSTITCH at each end.

FLIP OVER the tunic and REPEAT on the other side.

PRESS the seams OPEN and FLAT.

SEWING THE SIDE SEAMS (with pockets)

To ADD SIDE POCKETS to your tunic, TRACE off the SIDE POCKET piece from the pattern sheet. CUT out four pocket bags in a lightweight woven fabric. Poly-cotton is ideal. Make sure that you place and pin your pattern ON GRAIN (see page 22).

10 On the SIDE SEAMS, using tailor's chalk, MARK the points where you'd like the POCKET TOPS to be. They must be in the SAME POSITION on both sides of the FRONT and BACK panels, so use a measuring tape.

11 With your FRONT and BACK tunic panels RIGHT SIDES UP, lay the SIDE POCKETS on top with RIGHT SIDES TOGETHER. PIN.

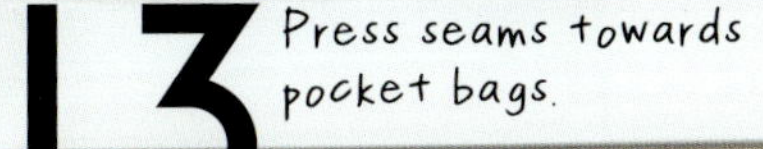

13 Press seams towards pocket bags.

Place Front and Back panels together and pin pocket bags.

Sew sides seams, pivot and stitch pocket bags. 15

12 With the EDGE of the PRESSER FOOT to the EDGE of the FABRIC, SEW all four pocket pieces to your tunic along the straight SIDE EDGES. ZIGZAG STITCH the straight RAW EDGES together to stop them from fraying.

13 PRESS the seams towards the pocket bags.

14 Place the front and back panels with RIGHT SIDES TOGETHER and match up the SIDE POCKETS. PIN the SIDE SEAMS and POCKET BAGS together. MARK the stitch line 1.5cm inside the side edges and around the pocket bags.

15 SEW the SIDE SEAMS from the armhole notch down. At the top of the pocket bags, PIVOT and STITCH around the curves of the POCKET BAGS. At the bottom of the pocket bags, PIVOT again and STITCH the rest of the SIDE SEAMS. ZIGZAG STITCH the RAW EDGES of the pocket bags to stop them fraying.

16 PRESS.

Your side pockets are complete!

16

Stitch round armhole edges.

18

Turn under 2cm all round hem and pin.

19

Sew hem with large zigzag stitches.

20

17

Turn under 1cm round armholes and pin.

FINISHING THE ARMHOLES

17 TURN UNDER 1cm all round both the ARMHOLE EDGES. PIN.

18 REMOVE the accessory tray from your sewing machine to reveal the free arm. SLIDE the tunic ARMHOLE onto the FREE ARM. Set your sewing machine to a large ZIGZAG STITCH. Starting at the SIDE SEAM, with the EDGE of the PRESSER FOOT to the EDGE of the FABRIC, STITCH all the way round the ARMHOLE EDGE.

FINISHING THE HEM

19 TURN UNDER at least 2cm all round the HEM EDGE to achieve the tunic length you require. PIN as shown.

20 Set your sewing machine to a large ZIGZAG STITCH. Using a sewing thread to match your fabric, starting and finishing at a side seam, SEW along the RAW HEM EDGE. STRETCH the fabric slightly both in FRONT and BEHIND the PRESSER FOOT to stop the hem from unfolding.

STEAM PRESS the hem and armhole edges.

If your hem line stretches during sewing, HOVER a STEAM IRON just above the fabric and STEAM WELL until the fabric gently SHRINKS back into place.

DESIGN
IDEA

How about adding a CONTRAST COLOUR NECKBAND to your tunic? Or what about making the FRONT panel in a RECYCLED WOVEN FABRIC and the BACK panel in a STRETCH FABRIC? You could use a VINTAGE CURTAIN or a LACE TABLECLOTH for the FRONT panel or even cut up some old DENIM JEANS and PATCHWORK the pieces together (see page 104). Instead of adding side pockets you could add PATCH POCKETS to the front, taken from a pair of old jeans (see page 113).

SIMPLE HAND PRINTING

Hand printing is great fun and a really easy way to add cool designs to your clothes.

YOU WILL NEED

- Mini paint roller and paint tray, from your local DIY centre
- Textile paint
- Newspaper
- Pins
- Apron (textile paint doesn't come off your clothes, so be careful)

Rip or cut shapes from newspaper and pin on fabric.

Roller textile paint over newspaper shapes and fabric.

Remove newspaper shapes and hang up to dry.

1 LAY out your PREPARED FABRIC on a flat work surface. Either RIP or CUT shapes out of NEWSPAPER and PIN them onto your FABRIC.

2 POUR a small amount of TEXTILE PAINT into the PAINT TRAY. Cover the MINI PAINT ROLLER with TEXTILE PAINT. Rolling from the CENTRE of the NEWSPAPER SHAPES towards the EDGES, completely COVER your FABRIC with paint. TIP: Don't put the paint on too thickly, as it may crack and fall off when dry.

3 Once painted, REMOVE the NEWSPAPER SHAPES and then HANG up the FABRIC to dry thoroughly.

When dry, the paint must be HEAT SEALED by using a hot iron on the REVERSE side of the fabric. WASH SEPARATELY on a cool cycle for the first few washes.

DESIGN IDEA

Swap textile paint for thick bleach. If your fabric has a high cotton content, this can look great. Always test a little swatch first. Be careful as bleach burns: wear rubber gloves and glasses, and work very slowly so the bleach doesn't splash onto your skin or clothing. If it does, immediately rinse off the bleach with water. Rinse well.

VINTAGE SCARF TOP

LEVEL 3 PROJECT

Collect as many gorgeous vintage scarves from carboot sales and charity shops as you can lay your hands on. They're inexpensive to buy and a great way of recycling textiles. Maybe your mum, grandma or auntie has a retro scarf from the 1960s, '70s or '80s hidden in a cupboard. Search for exotic or pretty florals for a summery feel, crazy paisleys for a bohemian festival vibe or geometric bold patterns for a cool sports look.

Team your vintage scarf with some stretch cotton jersey fabric for the back and sleeves. Choose a shade to match one of the colours in your print scarf. You could use a piece of printed fabric instead of a scarf or maybe cut up an old skirt or dress that you no longer wear and use that for the front panel instead.

- Dressmaker's pattern paper
- Print scarf or print fabric, large enough for front
- Lightweight stretch cotton jersey fabric, large enough for back, sleeves and neckband
- Universal needle for your sewing machine
- Sewing thread to match fabric
- Essential sewing equipment (see pages 12–13)

★★★★★★★★★★★★★★★★★★★★★★

For this project you need to use PATTERN B, which you'll find on the pattern sheet that comes with this book. Make sure you take your chest measurement first and use the correct size. TRACE off your size onto dressmaker's pattern paper. You need the FRONT BODICE, the BACK BODICE, the SLEEVE and the NECKBAND. If you want to make a cropped top, like mine, then fold along the lines marked on the FRONT and BACK panels to shorten them.

CUTTING OUT YOUR TOP

LAY out your print scarf or fabric and stretch cotton jersey fabric on a flat surface. FOLD the fabrics in half. Place the CENTRE line of your FRONT and BACK pattern pieces (where it says 'place on fold of fabric') exactly on the fabric FOLDS. PIN. Make sure that the pattern pieces are ON GRAIN (see page 22).

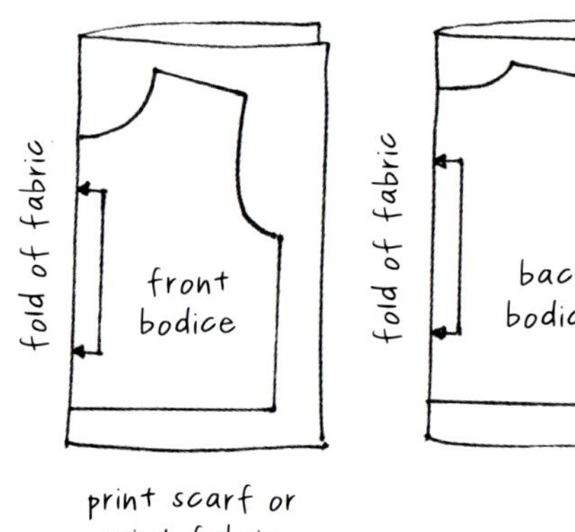

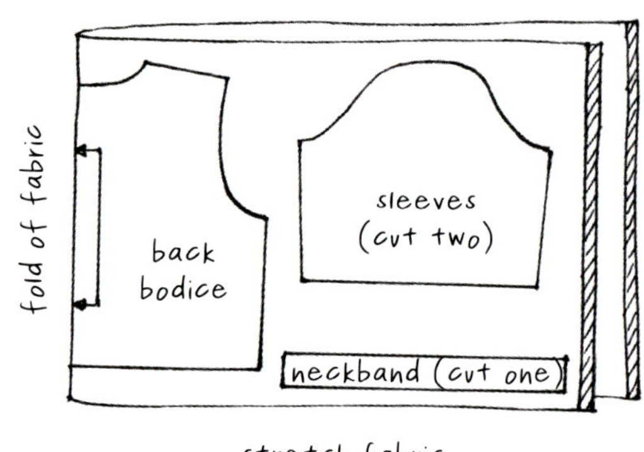

CUT out one FRONT BODICE from the PRINT scarf or fabric, then one BACK BODICE, two SLEEVES and one NECKBAND from the STRETCH fabric.

Using tailor's chalk, MARK the NOTCHES at the CENTRE of each SLEEVE HEAD on BOTH SIDES. MARK the MID-POINT NECKLINE on the FRONT for matching up the neckband.

SETTING UP YOUR SEWING MACHINE

FIT a sharp, new UNIVERSAL NEEDLE in your sewing machine.

Use a 1CM SEAM ALLOWANCE throughout for this top. As a guide, PLACE the RIGHT EDGE of the PRESSER FOOT on the RAW EDGE of the FABRIC or PLACE a STRIP of TAPE along the 1cm line on the BASE PLATE and use this to LINE UP the RAW EDGE of the FABRIC.

Always BACKSTITCH at the BEGINNING and END of every line of STITCHES.

ADDING THE BUST DARTS (for all sizes, except size 1)

If you have a bust and need to create BUST DARTS, do this NOW. Go to page 34 to learn how to do this. If you don't need to add bust darts to your top, go straight to step 1.

1 Pin and stitch one shoulder seam. Finish edges with zigzag.

2 Add neckband to neckline and pin and stitch second shoulder seam.

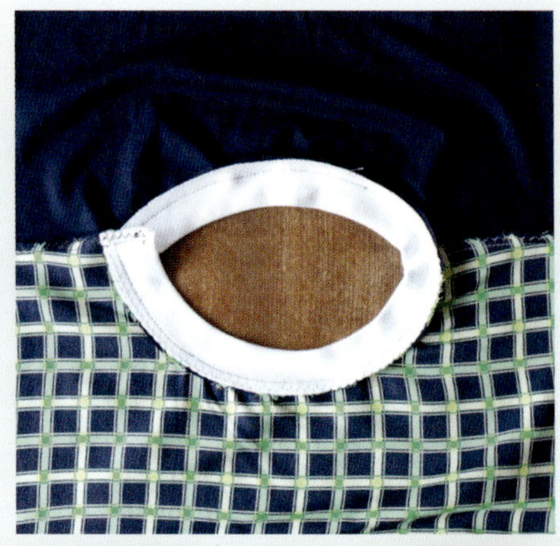
3 Finish raw edges with zigzag stitches to prevent fraying.

MAKING THE TOP

1 Place the FRONT and BACK panels RIGHT SIDES TOGETHER and PIN at one SHOULDER SEAM. Set your sewing machine to a STRAIGHT STITCH. With a 1cm seam allowance, with the FRONT panel ON TOP, SEW from the NECK edge to the ARMHOLE edge. BACKSTITCH at each end.

Set your sewing machine to a large ZIGZAG STITCH and FINISH the RAW EDGES to stop them fraying.

PRESS the shoulder seam towards the BACK of the top.

Now GO TO PAGE 118 to learn how to ADD THE NECKBAND to your NECKLINE.

2 Once the neckband has been attached, PIN the FRONT and BACK panels together at the second SHOULDER SEAM. Set your sewing machine to a STRAIGHT STITCH. SEW the shoulder seam. BACKSTITCH at each end.

3 FINISH the RAW EDGES with a large ZIGZAG STITCH to stop them from fraying.

PRESS the shoulder seam towards the back of the top.

Place sleeve heads in armholes, matching centre pins and seams.

Add pins to sleeve heads at right angles to edges.

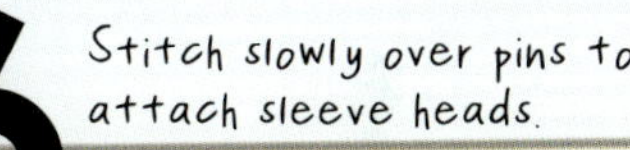

Stitch slowly over pins to attach sleeve heads.

ADDING THE SLEEVES

PLACE the top RIGHT SIDE UP.

4 LAY the SLEEVES on top of the ARMHOLES with RIGHT SIDES DOWN. MATCH up the CENTRE NOTCHES on the SLEEVE HEADS to the SHOULDER SEAMS. PIN as shown.

5 Next, PIN the ENDS of the SLEEVE HEADS to the CORNERS of the ARMHOLES.

ADD more PINS at RIGHT ANGLES to the EDGE. Space the pins 2cm apart, with their points just over the edge of the fabric. Make sure the two RAW EDGES are TOGETHER all the way along. Do NOT STRETCH the SLEEVE FABRIC as you pin.

6 Set your sewing machine to a STRAIGHT STRETCH STITCH or tiny ZIGZAG STITCH. With a 1cm seam allowance, SEW SLOWLY over the pins along the sleeve heads. Keep checking that there are NO PLEATS forming UNDERNEATH your sewing. STRETCH the fabric slightly both in FRONT of and BEHIND the PRESSER FOOT to keep it flat.

REMOVE the PINS. FINISH the RAW EDGES with a large ZIGZAG STITCH to stop them from fraying.

PRESS the seam allowances towards the BODY of the top.

Pin and stitch underarm sleeve and side seams.

7

Turn under 1-2cm all round cuffs and hem. Pin.

8

Sew cuffs and hem with large zigzag stitches.

TIP

If your sewing machine skips any stitches when stitching the stretch fabric, change from a universal needle to a STRETCH NEEDLE.

SEWING THE SIDE SEAMS

With RIGHT SIDES TOGETHER, PIN along the entire length of the UNDERARM SLEEVE SEAMS and SIDE SEAMS from CUFF EDGES to HEMS.

7 Set your sewing machine to a STRAIGHT STRETCH STITCH. With a 1cm seam allowance, SEW from the CUFF to the HEM. BACKSTITCH at each end.

FINISH the RAW EDGES with a large ZIGZAG STITCH to stop them from fraying. PRESS the side seams towards the back.

FINISHING THE CUFFS AND HEM

8 TURN UNDER 1–2cm all round the HEM and CUFF EDGES. PIN. Use a measuring tape to keep your hems even.

9 REMOVE the accessory tray from your sewing machine to reveal the free arm. SLIDE the TOP onto the FREE ARM. Set your sewing machine to a large ZIGZAG STITCH. Starting at a SIDE SEAM, with a 1cm seam allowance, SEW all the way round the HEM. STRETCH the fabric slightly both in FRONT and BEHIND the PRESSER FOOT to keep it flat.

REPEAT for the CUFFS, starting at the UNDERARM SEAM.

STEAM PRESS the hem and cuffs to shrink any stretching.

Make a longer version of the Vintage Scarf Top to wear as a dress, over leggings, with jeans or just with sandals during the summer. To go with the print top, you could also make a matching skater skirt using several more scarves and create a co-ordinating set.

DENIM DUNGAREE DRESS

The dungaree dress, pinafore dress, bib and braces... call it what you will, this is a hot trend that's set to last. This dress is versatile and can be worn all year round – with a T-shirt and flip-flops in summer or a sweater and boots in winter. You could add embroidery or appliqué patchwork to the finished panels? Or if you prefer, just make a skirt without the bib.

As we love to recycle at The Fashion Factory, all you need is a few pairs of jeans. You can buy worn denims cheaply at carboot sales. Look for medium- to lightweight denim in large sizes (not kids'), so there's plenty of usable fabric.

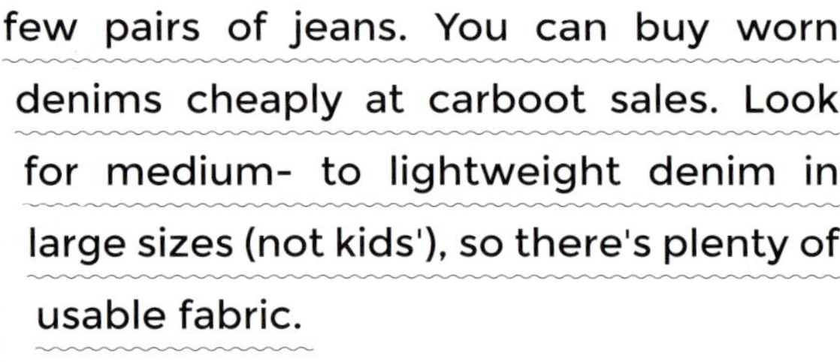

Colours are important, so think about the mix of denim; you'll realise how many different shades jeans come in. It's fine for the denim to have a little bit of stretch in it – a lot of denim does – but avoid anything very stretchy, as this may affect how the dress hangs.

RECYCLED JEANS

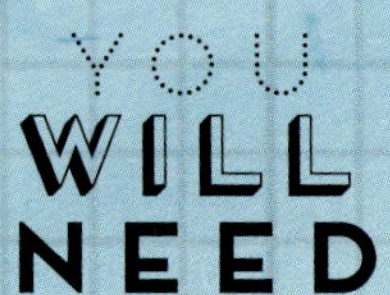

For this project you need to use the DENIM DUNGAREE DRESS BIB PATTERN, which you'll find on the pattern sheet that comes with this book. You also need to use a SKIRT PATTERN that you make yourself. Go to page 16 to learn how to do this. Don't forget the waistband pattern as well.

- Dressmaker's pattern paper
- 2 or 3 pairs of jeans in medium- or lightweight denim in adults' sizes
- Sewing thread to match fabric
- 15cm closed-end zip with metal teeth (check it works)
- Sewing thread to match zip
- Jumbo snap fasteners OR dungaree slides and buttons
- Universal needle for sewing machine
- Essential sewing equipment (see pages 12–13)

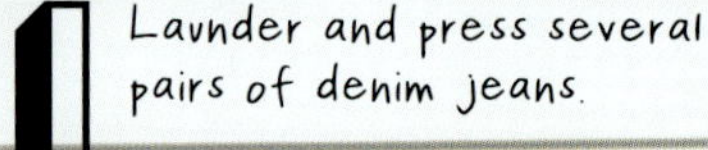

1 Launder and press several pairs of denim jeans.

Cut across front of right leg with sharp scissors. 2

SETTING UP YOUR SEWING MACHINE

FIT a new UNIVERSAL NEEDLE in your sewing machine.

Use a 1.5CM SEAM ALLOWANCE for this dress unless otherwise stated. As a guide, PLACE a STRIP of TAPE along the 1.5cm line on the BASE PLATE and use this to LINE UP the RAW EDGE of the FABRIC.

Always BACKSTITCH at the BEGINNING and END of every line of STITCHES.

PREPARING THE DENIM FABRIC

1 Make sure all the POCKETS of each pair of JEANS are EMPTY. PLACE the jeans in the WASHING MACHINE for a fairly HOT WASH, if they need it. When dry, give them a good STEAM PRESS with an iron to REMOVE as many CREASES as possible.

2 CUT OFF the LEGS of the jeans, leaving large panels of USABLE FABRIC. Using sharp fabric scissors, CUT across the FRONT of the RIGHT LEG as high up as possible, in an arch shape.

Turn jeans over and cut across back of leg.

3

Cut down outside seam to open out leg.

4

5

Trim away thick outside edge seams and press.

6

Repeat with more jeans if you need more fabric.

3 **TURN THE JEANS OVER** and **CUT** across the **BACK** of the **RIGHT LEG**, just **UNDER** the **BACK POCKETS**. This will release the right leg.

4 **CUT OPEN** along the thick **OUTSIDE LEG SEAM** to open it out into a **FLAT PANEL** of denim. Do **NOT** cut open the inside leg seam.

5 **REMOVE THE OUTSIDE SEAM** by trimming off the thick seams and seam allowances, leaving smooth, flat edges. **STEAM PRESS** the panel with a hot iron to **REMOVE** as many **CREASES** as possible.

6 **REPEAT** with the **LEFT LEG**. If you want to include other colours of denim, you'll need to do this with each pair. Do **NOT** throw away your fabric scraps.

7 Lay skirt pattern piece on top of denim panel.

8 Pin on another denim panel until it's big enough.

Draw round your pattern piece and cut out.

PREPARING THE SKIRT PANELS

7 TAKE a large DENIM PANEL and PIN a SECOND piece to the EDGE. OVERLAP it by a couple of centimetres. PIN.

8 LAY your SKIRT PATTERN PIECE on top. Is the denim big enough? If not, ADD MORE PANELS. It looks best when the panels run diagonally across the skirt.

9 LAY your SKIRT PATTERN PIECE on top of your pinned DENIM PANELS. PIN the pattern down and, using a fibre-tip pen, carefully DRAW around the EDGE of the PATTERN. Remove the pattern piece to reveal the skirt outline and roughly cut it out a little bigger all the way around.

Set your sewing machine to a medium/large ZIGZAG STITCH. Sewing on the right side, TOPSTITCH along the EDGES of the PANELS to join them together. Do NOT leave any GAPS. BACKSTITCH each row of stitches just inside the outline.

TIP

Choose your sewing thread colour. I prefer to use a matching shade, like a blue or a grey, so the stitches don't show too much. If you want to add colour, you can do that when your skirt panels are complete.

Trim away any excess denim from seam allowances on reverse.

Zigzag stitch around skirt outline and carefully cut out.

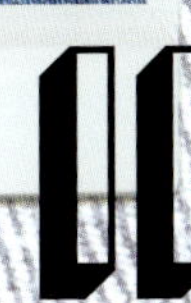

10 When all the denim pieces are stitched together, FLIP the skirt panel over and check that there are NO GAPS in your stitching. TRIM away any EXCESS denim from the back of the seams to neaten.

Give the skirt panel a really good STEAM PRESS with a very hot iron. Using steam helps to shrink back any stretching that has happened during stitching.

11 SEW a line of ZIGZAG STITCHES just INSIDE your SKIRT OUTLINE, all the way round your skirt shape. Take it slowly, stitch carefully and PIVOT neatly at the corners. STEAM PRESS well to reduce any stretching along the edges.

Now CUT OUT the skirt panel along your pen OUTLINE.

That's the first skirt panel done!

Now REPEAT steps 7-11 to make a SECOND SKIRT PANEL. Decide which panel you like best; that's the one you'll use for the FRONT of your skirt.

If you're adding any detail to your skirt panels, such as embroidery, appliqué or pockets then now is the time to do so. Go to the sections on pages 46, 94 and 102 to learn how to do this. Once you're done, give the skirt panels a good steam press and continue to follow these instructions from step 12.

12 Cut out waistband strip from another denim panel.

13 Stitch front and back skirt panels together along one side seam.

14 Finish seam allowances with zigzag stitching.

PREPARING THE WAISTBAND

(12) Place your WAISTBAND PATTERN PIECE on a long, flat panel of denim fabric. PIN and CUT it out.

MAKING THE SKIRT

Set your sewing machine to a regular STRAIGHT STITCH. SEW a line of STRAIGHT STITCHES 1cm in from the waist edge on both skirt panels. BACKSTITCH at each end. This is called STAY STITCHING and stops the waistline from stretching.

STEAM PRESS the panels flat.

(13) PLACE your skirt panels with RIGHT SIDES TOGETHER. PIN along one SIDE SEAM.

Using a regular STRAIGHT STITCH and a 1.5cm SEAM ALLOWANCE, SEW the SIDE SEAM from the WAIST down to the HEM. BACKSTITCH at each end.

(14) Set your sewing machine to a large ZIGZAG STITCH and finish the raw edges of the seam allowance.

STEAM PRESS the seam open and flat.

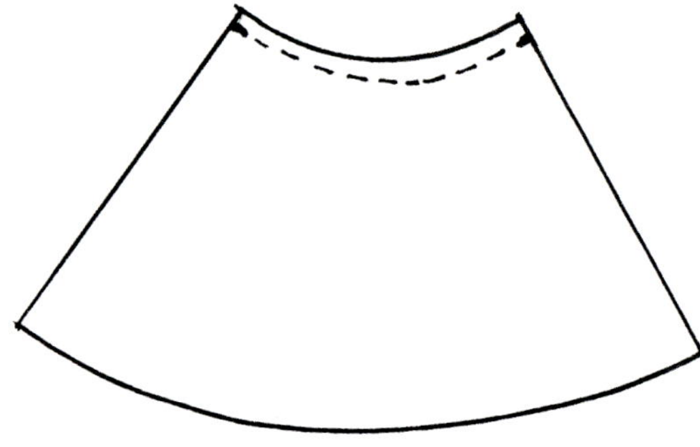

15 Pin waistband to right side of skirt.

16

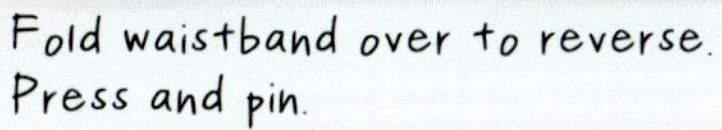

Fold waistband over to reverse. Press and pin.

Zigzag stitch through all layers.

17

ATTACHING THE WAISTBAND

15 PLACE your skirt RIGHT SIDE UP. LAY the WAISTBAND on top RIGHT SIDE DOWN against the WAIST EDGE of the skirt. PLACE the two RAW EDGES TOGETHER. Starting at the left side, PIN all the way along.

Set your sewing machine to a regular STRAIGHT STITCH. SEW all the way along. Keep checking that there are NO PLEATS forming UNDERNEATH your sewing. BACKSTITCH at each end. STEAM PRESS the seam allowance upwards.

Using a large ZIGZAG STITCH, sew along the other RAW EDGE of the WAISTBAND to stop it from fraying. STEAM PRESS flat.

16 FOLD the WAISTBAND over and STEAM PRESS so it just covers the row of STRAIGHT STITCHING at the waist (by about 1cm). Make a sharp CREASE along the TOP EDGE of the WAISTBAND.

With the skirt RIGHT SIDE UP, PIN through all of the layers just ABOVE the WAIST SEAM.

17 Using a large ZIGZAG STITCH (or an embroidery stitch, if you prefer), SEW all the way along on the EDGE of the WAISTBAND. Sew slowly and keep your stitching neat.

STEAM PRESS flat.

TIP

If you get stuck on the waistband seam, where there are lots of layers of fabric, try gently pulling the fabric from the back of the presser foot or manually turning the machine handwheel towards you. If your sewing machine misses a few stitches because of the fabric thickness, just backstitch over the missed area.

18 Pin and stitch second side seam.

19 Press seam open and flat.

Lay zip on top of side seam and pin in place.

20

STITCHING THE SIDE SEAM

18 FOLD your skirt panels in HALF with RIGHT SIDES TOGETHER. PIN the second SIDE SEAM from the WAIST to HEM.

Using a regular STRAIGHT STITCH and a 1.5cm SEAM ALLOWANCE, sew the SIDE SEAM from the WAIST to the HEM. BACKSTITCH at each end.

STEAM PRESS the seam OPEN and FLAT.

19 Set your sewing machine to a large ZIGZAG STITCH and finish the raw edges of the seam allowance. STEAM PRESS the seam open.

ADDING THE SIDE ZIP

20 Turn the skirt so it is RIGHT SIDE OUT. LAY your ZIP on top of the SIDE SEAM. FOLD OVER the TOP of the ZIP TAPE inside the skirt and PIN all the way down one side to the END of the ZIP. Make sure that the teeth of the ZIP sit exactly on the SEAM LINE all the way down.

OPEN the zip HALF WAY.

Thread your sewing machine with a colour to match your zip tape.

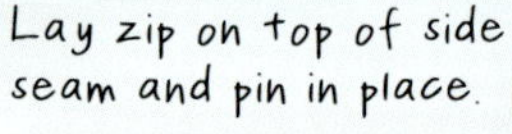

21

Zigzag stitch zip tape with presser foot against metal teeth.

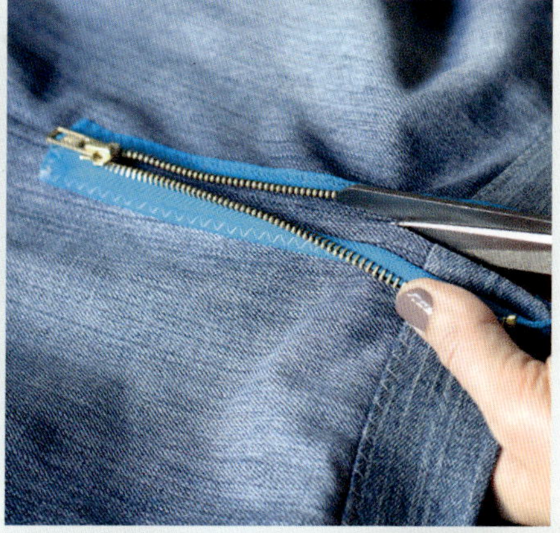

Open zip and cut along side seam behind zip.

(21) Set your sewing machine to a large ZIGZAG STITCH.

PLACE the LEFT SIDE of the PRESSER FOOT against the side of the metal ZIP TEETH. BACKSTITCH and then SEW from the TOP down to the ZIP PULL.

TURN the HANDWHEEL of your machine towards you until the POINT of the NEEDLE is through the FABRIC. LIFT the PRESSER FOOT and CLOSE the ZIP.

LOWER the PRESSER FOOT and continue sewing to the END of the ZIP. Keep the PRESSER FOOT against the side of the metal ZIP TEETH at all times. BACKSTITCH at the end.

REPEAT on the OTHER SIDE of the ZIP.

SEW a row of ZIGZAG STITCHES across the BOTTOM END of the ZIP TAPE twice. BACKSTITCH well. TRIM all the THREADS.

(22) OPEN the zip ALL THE WAY. Using a seam ripper or sharp fabric scissors, CUT the SIDE SEAM open behind the zip. STOP at the ZIP PULL.

STEAM PRESS the zip flat on the reverse side.

TIP

If your denim is thick or you find it tricky to keep the zip tape turned over at the top of the zip when sewing, leave it open and hand stitch it down with just a couple of stitches afterwards.

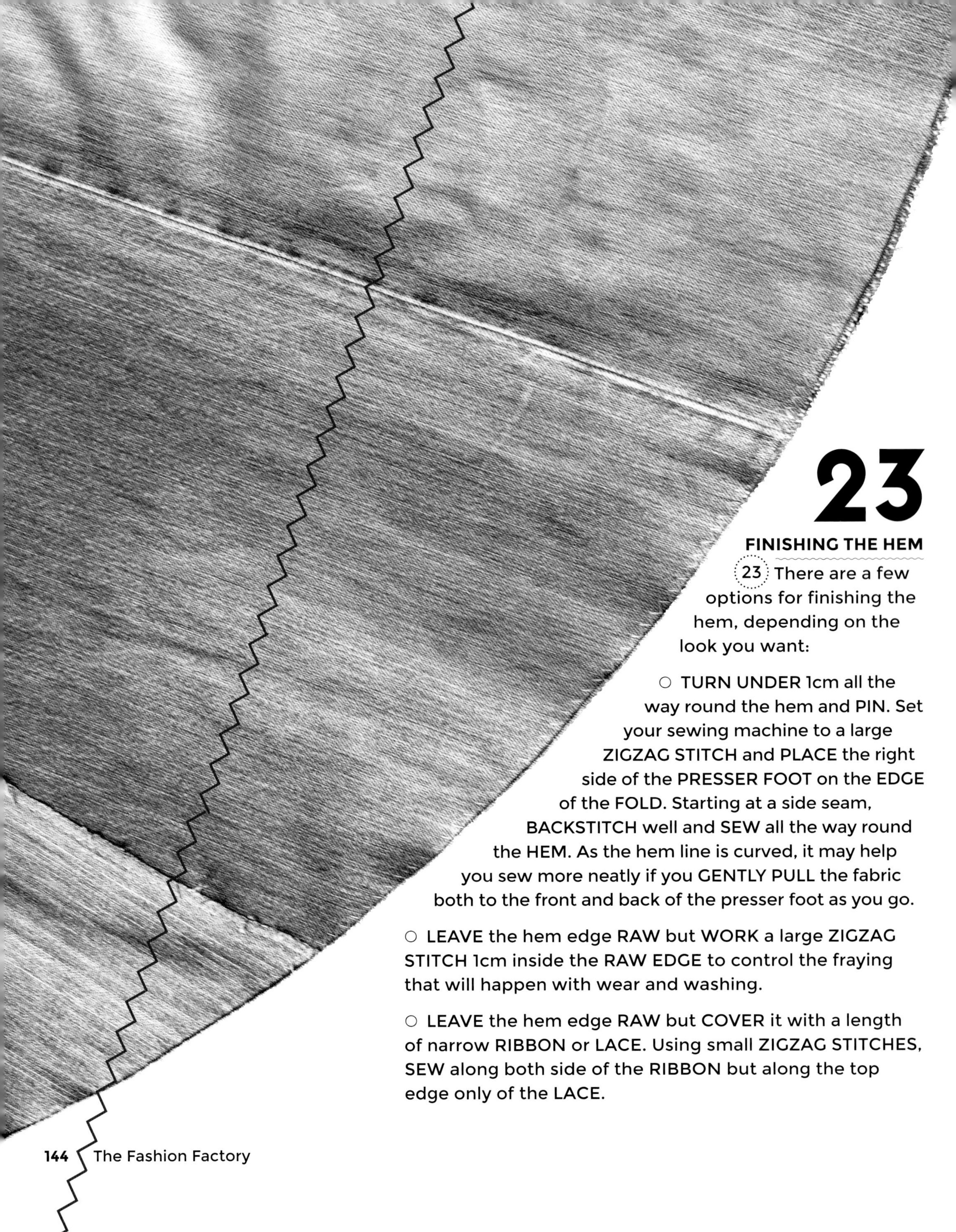

23

FINISHING THE HEM

23 There are a few options for finishing the hem, depending on the look you want:

- TURN UNDER 1cm all the way round the hem and PIN. Set your sewing machine to a large ZIGZAG STITCH and PLACE the right side of the PRESSER FOOT on the EDGE of the FOLD. Starting at a side seam, BACKSTITCH well and SEW all the way round the HEM. As the hem line is curved, it may help you sew more neatly if you GENTLY PULL the fabric both to the front and back of the presser foot as you go.
- LEAVE the hem edge RAW but WORK a large ZIGZAG STITCH 1cm inside the RAW EDGE to control the fraying that will happen with wear and washing.
- LEAVE the hem edge RAW but COVER it with a length of narrow RIBBON or LACE. Using small ZIGZAG STITCHES, SEW along both side of the RIBBON but along the top edge only of the LACE.

24

Pin turnings around three edges of bib.

25

Sew down turnings around three edges of bib.

26

Mark centre fronts of bib and skirt with pins.

MAKING AND ATTACHING THE BIB

Using the BIB PATTERN PIECE, create a full bib. Either FOLD a panel of denim in half, place the pattern piece against the fold and CUT OUT ONE WHOLE BIB panel OR take a FLAT panel of denim, use the pattern piece to CUT OUT TWO HALF BIB panels (one reversed) and join them along the centre front. ZIGZAG STITCH your seam edges and STEAM PRESS them open.

24 Place the bib RIGHT SIDE DOWN. Using a ruler, FOLD under and PRESS the SIDE EDGES to the wrong side by 1.5cm. FOLD under and PRESS the TOP EDGE by 2cm. PIN the edges, noting the direction of the pins.

25 Starting at the bottom corner and using a large ZIGZAG STITCH, sew along the INSIDE RAW EDGES of the turnings. STEAM PRESS.

26 PLACE your BIB and SKIRT on a flat surface RIGHT SIDE UP and with the ZIP to the SIDE. Using a measuring tape, MARK the CENTRE FRONT of the bib and skirt with a pin.

If you're adding any decorative detail or a pocket, now is the time to do it.

Tuck bib inside waistband and pin, matching centre front points.

28

Zigzag stitch bib to waistband of skirt.

27 TUCK the bib BEHIND the WAISTBAND of the skirt. MATCH up the CENTRE FRONT POINTS of the BIB and SKIRT using the marker pins. PIN the BIB to the WAISTBAND, noting the direction of the pins.

TRY ON your dungaree dress to make sure that the BIB is in the CORRECT POSITION. The top of the bib should just cover your chest. Lower it if the bib is too big.

28 REMOVE the accessory tray from your sewing machine and SLIDE the SKIRT onto the FREE ARM. Using a large ZIGZAG STITCH, sew the bib to the skirt. BACKSTITCH well at each end. If you prefer, continue your stitching all the way round the top of the waistband, avoiding the top of the zip.

STEAM PRESS.

You're nearly done. Just the straps to do.

29

Draw two 6cm wide strips on reverse of a denim panel.

30

Cut out two 6cm-wide strips that are equal size.

31 Fold and press sides of each strip into centre.

MAKING AND ATTACHING THE STRAPS AND FINISHING

PUT on your dungaree dress. PIN the BIB to the TOP you're already wearing to hold it in place. Ask someone else to MEASURE the distance from the TOP EDGE of the BIB to the BACK POINT, over your shoulders to the top edge of the waistband on the back of the skirt. ADD 10cm to this MEASUREMENT and make a note of it.

(29) Using a felt-tip pen and ruler, DRAW OUT TWO STRIPS, 6cm-wide, the same length as this measurement onto the reverse of a denim panel.

(30) CUT OUT these two 6cm-wide strips of denim, making sure they are equal size.

(31) FOLD and PRESS the SIDES of each strip TOWARDS the CENTRE so that they almost touch. Do this all the way down both strips.

STEAM PRESS flat.

32

Zigzag stitch along long edges of straps.

33

Find centre back point of skirt and mark with a pin.

34

Pin straps to waist, cross over at back and pin to bib.

(32) Using a large ZIGZAG STITCH, sew along both LONG EDGES of each strap. To keep it neat, place the EDGE of the PRESSER FOOT to the EDGE of the FOLD. BACKSTITCH at each end.

STEAM PRESS flat.

(33) LAY the dungaree dress RIGHT SIDE DOWN. Using a measuring tape, find the CENTRE BACK POINT and MARK with a PIN.

(34) On either side of the CENTRE BACK POINT, pin one STRAP to the WRONG SIDE of the WAISTBAND, overlapping by NO MORE than 2cm. The gap between the strap ends should be between 5cm and 8cm. CROSS the straps over and roughly PIN the other ends to the bib at a SLIGHT ANGLE.

TRY on the dungaree dress with the straps over your shoulders. CHECK that the straps are sitting properly at the back and are the right length. If not, adjust them or ask someone else to pin them in the right place for you.

Zigzag stitch strap ends in place on waistband at back.

Add dungaree slides and shank buttons to straps and bib.

Hand stitch jumbo snap fasteners to straps and bib.

37

35 Using a ZIGZAG or STRAIGHT STITCH, sew the strap ends to the waistband. BACKSTITCH at each end.

36 To attach the straps to your dungaree dress you can use DUNGAREE SLIDES, like the ones shown. PLACE the SLIDES onto the STRAPS. Then ADD BUTTONS to the BIB for the slides to hook on to. Sew them on well. Once the buttons are in place, fold your straps back and stitch them down to hold the slide in place.

37 The other way to attach the straps to your dungaree dress is to use JUMBO SNAP FASTENERS.
These are easy to handstitch onto the ends of your straps. It's best to put the dress on and mark the position of the fasteners first with pins or a pen. STITCH well through EACH HOLE, making sure that your stitches don't come through to the right side of the fabric.

You've finished. Rock your new look!

MACHINE EMBROIDERY

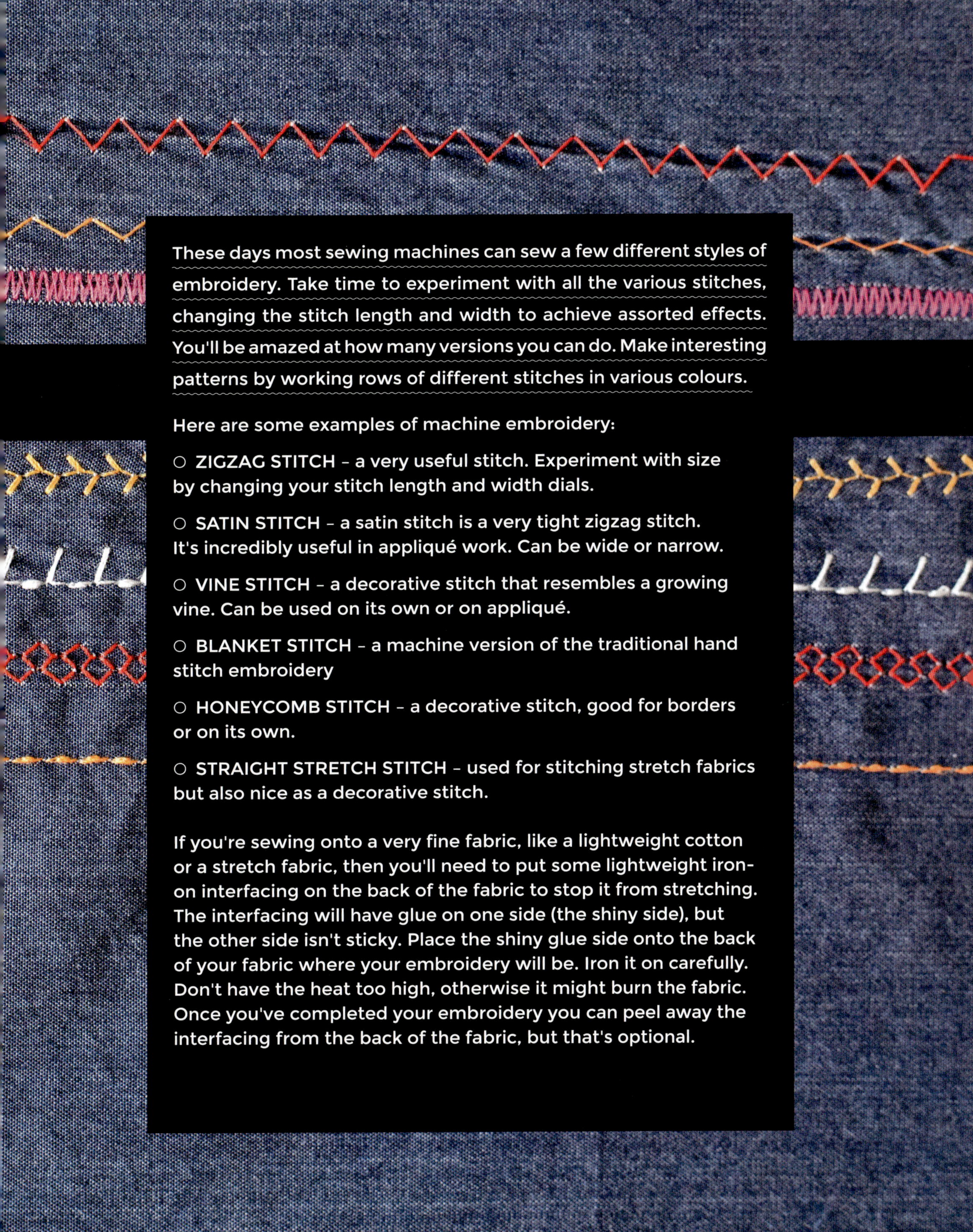

These days most sewing machines can sew a few different styles of embroidery. Take time to experiment with all the various stitches, changing the stitch length and width to achieve assorted effects. You'll be amazed at how many versions you can do. Make interesting patterns by working rows of different stitches in various colours.

Here are some examples of machine embroidery:

○ ZIGZAG STITCH – a very useful stitch. Experiment with size by changing your stitch length and width dials.

○ SATIN STITCH – a satin stitch is a very tight zigzag stitch. It's incredibly useful in appliqué work. Can be wide or narrow.

○ VINE STITCH – a decorative stitch that resembles a growing vine. Can be used on its own or on appliqué.

○ BLANKET STITCH – a machine version of the traditional hand stitch embroidery

○ HONEYCOMB STITCH – a decorative stitch, good for borders or on its own.

○ STRAIGHT STRETCH STITCH – used for stitching stretch fabrics but also nice as a decorative stitch.

If you're sewing onto a very fine fabric, like a lightweight cotton or a stretch fabric, then you'll need to put some lightweight iron-on interfacing on the back of the fabric to stop it from stretching. The interfacing will have glue on one side (the shiny side), but the other side isn't sticky. Place the shiny glue side onto the back of your fabric where your embroidery will be. Iron it on carefully. Don't have the heat too high, otherwise it might burn the fabric. Once you've completed your embroidery you can peel away the interfacing from the back of the fabric, but that's optional.

UPCYCLED KNITWEAR BEANIE

LEVEL 2 PROJECT

Don't throw away your old knitwear! Make yourself, your family and your friends cool and cosy beanie hats. Chunky knitwear is great for this project, or if you're using a finer knit fabric you can add a fab lining with a bit of stretch fabric and make the hat reversible. You could add a badge to the front (see page 80) or a pompom on top. Or how about some animal ears? Just experiment. Here's how...

1 Pin top dart and stitch.

2 Pin centre back seam and stitch.

3 Pin round top curve and stitch.

4 Turn finished beanie right side out.

SUITABLE FOR CHUNKY KNITS

MAKING A BASIC BEANIE HAT (without lining)

TRACE off the BEANIE HAT pattern from the sheet that comes with this book.

TAKE an OLD SWEATER and CUT off the SLEEVES at the armhole seams. (These can make great leg warmers - see page 155). CUT OPEN the SHOULDER SEAMS and CUT ALONG one SIDE SEAM. LAY out the cut sweater FLAT. If you're using a cardigan, just open it up and it lay out flat.

PLACE the BOTTOM EDGE of the BEANIE HAT paper pattern on the BOTTOM EDGE of the KNIT FABRIC. PIN. Carefully CUT out the BEANIE HAT.

1 PIN the top DART with RIGHT SIDES TOGETHER. Start sewing right on the FOLDED EDGE (1cm below the cut edge as marked on pattern). STITCH.

2 PIN the CENTRE BACK SEAM together and STITCH, with a 1cm seam allowance. Gently STEAM PRESS the seam open.

3 With the CENTRE BACK SEAM in the middle, PIN round the TOP CURVE. Start sewing right on the FOLDED EDGE (1cm below the cut edge). STITCH.

4 Turn out the right way.

That's your basic beanie done!

Use a small ZIGZAG STITCH to sew the beanie together. Place the RIGHT EDGE of the presser foot to the RAW EDGE of the knit on EVERY SEAM. Remember to BACKSTITCH at the BEGINNING and END of EVERY SEAM.

1 Make up a knit fabric and a stretch fabric beanie.

2 Place stretch fabric beanie inside knit fabric beanie and pin.

3 Zigzag stitch around bottom edge to join layers, leaving a gap.

4 Push stretch fabric lining inside hat. Hand stitch gap closed.

MAKING A REVERSIBLE BEANIE HAT (with lining)

1 FOLLOW STEPS 1–4 on page 153 with both your KNIT FABRIC and your STRETCH FABRIC, noting the DIRECTION OF STRETCH marked on the pattern piece.

2 With the KNIT BEANIE INSIDE OUT and the FABRIC BEANIE RIGHT SIDE OUT, PLACE the FABRIC BEANIE inside the KNIT BEANIE. MATCH UP the CENTRE BACK SEAMS. PIN all the way round the HEM.

3 REMOVE the accessory tray from your sewing machine to expose the free arm. Using a medium ZIGZAG STITCH, sew all the way round the EDGE of both beanies, leaving open a GAP of approximately 6cm. Gently STRETCH the two layers as you sew. BACKSTITCH either side of the gap.

4 TURN the whole hat out the other way THROUGH the GAP. PUSH the STRETCH FABRIC LINING inside the hat. Neatly HAND STITCH the GAP closed. Trim all your threads.

That's your reversible beanie done!

Hand sew running stitches around circle of fun fur fabric.

Pull thread to gather pompom and fill with wadding.

2

Pull thread tight, stitch pompom closed and attach to hat.

3

ADDING A FUN FUR POMPOM

1 CUT out a CIRCLE of FUN FUR FABRIC 15cm in diameter.

THREAD UP a hand-sewing needle, DOUBLE your THREAD and tie a KNOT in the END.

Working from the BACK, SEW small RUNNING STITCHES (1cm long) all the way round the INSIDE EDGE of the FUR.

2 When you return to the start, gently PULL the THREAD to GATHER the EDGES. LEAVE a small HOLE at the CENTRE.

FILL the gathered pompom with POLYESTER WADDING or tiny cuttings of an old sweater or some tights.

PULL the THREAD tight, leaving a HOLE 2cm in diameter. STITCH over and over ON THE SPOT (and through the backing fabric) a few times to FIX the HOLE.

3 PUSH the top of the BEANIE HAT inside the HOLE, just a little. HOLD in place and STITCH well. SEW all the way round the POMPOM BASE. To finish, SEW three TINY STITCHES exactly ON TOP OF EACH OTHER so that the thread doesn't come undone.

Happy wearing!

MATCHING LEG WARMERS

1. CUT off your sweater sleeves STRAIGHT across the top.
2. TURN UNDER 1cm all round the top edge. PIN.
3. SEW two rows of SHIRRING ELASTIC around each end. Go to page 64 to learn how to do this.

INDEX 

Publishing Director Sarah Lavelle
Commissioning Editor Lisa Pendreigh
Editorial Assistant Harriet Butt
Creative Director Helen Lewis
Art Director & Designer Claire Peters
Photographers Alexandra Davenport, Chris Moore, Amanda Riley and Ellie Smith
Production Director Vincent Smith
Production Controller Tom Moore

First published in 2015 by
Quadrille Publishing Ltd
Pentagon House
52–54 Southwark Street
London SE1 1UN
www.quadrille.co.uk

Quadrille is an imprint of Hardie Grant.
www.hardiegrant.com.au

Quadrille craft

www.quadrillecraft.com

If you have any comments or queries regarding the instructions in this book, please contact us at enquiries@quadrille.co.uk

Photography
Amanda Riley pages 1, 7, 8, 11, 14–23, 26–27, 38–39, 71, 96–97, 124, 128–129, 133; Alexandra Davenport pages 12–13, 24–25, 30–35, 42–45, 54–59, 63–67, 69–70, 72, 74–75, 80–81, 84–85, 90–93, 100–101, 110–113, 118–122, 130–132, 136–139, 142–145, 150–155; Alexandra Davenport, Chris Moore pages 2–3, 68; Alexandra Davenport, Amanda Riley pages 41, 51, 53, 61, 73, 76–79, 82–83, 86–89, 94–95, 98–99, 102–105, 108–109, 114–117, 125, 127, 140–141; Ellie Smith pages 60, 62, 134; Alexandra Davenport, Ellie Smith pages 50, 146–149; Alexandra Davenport, Amanda Riley, Ellie Smith page 135

Cover photography
Alexandra Davenport, Chris Moore, Amanda Riley, Ellie Smith

British Library Cataloguing-in-Publication Data
A catalogue record for this book is available from the British Library.

ISBN: 978 1 84949 554 7

Printed in China

WITH THANKS TO...

My grandmother Ruby, who gave an 8 year old something to do and something to aspire to.

My mother Rosemary for passing on to me creative and artistic talent.

My junior school art teacher, Miss Caneaux at Eastlands School, who helped me realise creativity in a harsh landscape. You were my ray of sunshine.

My BTEC fashion tutors at East Warwickshire College, Pat, Pat, Sally and Val. Those were great days indeed.

My Kingston University fashion tutors who saw my potential and let me in.

Friends and family for putting up with my creative temperament and those who helped out at catwalk shows. Your help and support has been vital and is very much appreciated: Darren, Paul, Delphi, Tabs, Amanda, Alison, Helena, Mel, Katie, India, Zoe and to everyone involved.

Missy and Sandra at The 20th Century Theatre in Notting Hill, London, for allowing us to host our catwalk shows in your beautiful venue.

All my students at The Fashion Facotry, past and present. Keep up the creativity!

Lisa, Claire, Alex and Tom at Quadrille Publishing for helping me to construct this fabulous book. It's been a journey.

Elliot for being a wonderful and patient son and Sancho Panza just for being.

#THEFASHION FACTORY

PATTERN SHEET